ON BOARD.

Thomas Nickerson made his way down to his bunk and its mattress full of mildewed corn husks. As he faded off to sleep on the gently rocking ship, he surely felt what one young whaleman described as a great, almost overwhelming "pride in my floating home."

That night he was probably unaware of the latest bit of gossip circulating through town—of the strange goings-on out on the Commons. Swarms of grasshoppers had begun to appear in the turnip fields. "[T]he whole face of the earth has been spotted with them . . . ," Obed Macy would write. "[N]o person living ever knew them so numerous." A comet in July and now a plague of locusts?

As it turned out, things would end up badly for the two ships anchored off the Nantucket Bar on the evening of August 11, 1819. The *Chili* would not return for another three and a half years, and then with only five hundred barrels of sperm oil, about a quarter of what was needed to fill a ship her size. For Captain Coffin and his men, it would be a disastrous voyage.

But nothing could compare to what fate had in store for the twenty-one men of the *Essex*.

➤   ➤   ➤

"[Readers] who long for adventure or have an interest in historical fiction will enjoy this book because of its graphic and historical detail."
— *VOYA*

OTHER BOOKS YOU MAY ENJOY

REVENGE
OF THE
WHALE

NATHANIEL PHILBRICK

Revenge
OF THE
Whale

THE
TRUE STORY
OF THE
WHALESHIP
ESSEX

PUFFIN BOOKS
An Imprint of Penguin Group (USA)

PUFFIN BOOKS
Published by the Penguin Group
Penguin Group (USA) LLC
375 Hudson Street
New York, New York 10014

USA * Canada * UK * Ireland * Australia
New Zealand * India * South Africa * China

penguin.com
A Penguin Random House Company

First published in the United States of America by G. P. Putnam's Sons,
a division of Penguin Putnam Books for Young Readers, 2002
Published by Puffin Books, a division of Penguin Young Readers Group, 2004

THE LIBRARY OF CONGRESS HAS CATALOGED THE G. P. PUTNAM'S SONS EDITION AS FOLLOWS:
Philbrick, Nat.
Revenge of the whale: the true story of the whaleship Essex / Nathaniel Philbrick.
p. cm. Summary: Recounts the 1820 sinking of the whaleship "Essex" by an enraged
sperm whale and how the crew of young men survived against impossible odds.
Based on the author's adult book "In the Heart of the Sea."
Includes bibliographical references (p. 161).
ISBN (hardcover) 0-399-23795-X
1. Essex (Whaleship)—Juvenile literature. 2. Shipwrecks—Pacific Ocean—
Juvenile literature.
[1. Essex (Whaleship). 2. Shipwrecks. 3. Whaling. 4. Survival.] I. Title.
G530.E77 P46 2002 910'.9164—dc21 2002000667

Puffin Books ISBN 978-0-14-240068-5

Printed in the United States of America

19 20 18

To Melissa

REVENGE
OF THE
WHALE

Contents

Illustrations appear on pages v, 17, 34, 56–57, and 140.
Maps appear on pages 26–27 and 125.
Gallery of photographs follows page 68.

CREW OF THE *ESSEX*

CAPTAIN
George Pollard, Jr.

FIRST MATE
Owen Chase

SECOND MATE
Matthew Joy

BOATSTEERERS
Benjamin Lawrence • Obed Hendricks
Thomas Chappel

STEWARD
William Bond

SAILORS
Owen Coffin • Isaac Cole • Henry DeWitt
Richard Peterson • Charles Ramsdell • Barzillai Ray
Samuel Reed • Isaiah Sheppard • Charles Shorter
Lawson Thomas • Seth Weeks • Joseph West
William Wright

CABIN BOY
Thomas Nickerson

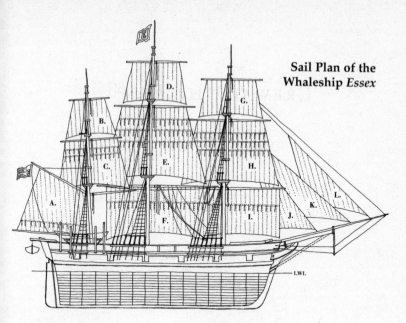

Sail Plan of the Whaleship *Essex*

A. mizzen sail
B. mizzen topgallant sail
C. mizzen topsail
D. main topgallant sail
E. main topsail
F. main course or mainsail

G. fore topgallant sail
H. fore topsail
I. fore course or fore sail
J. fore topmast staysail
K. jib
L. flying jib

Deck Plan of the Whaleship *Essex*

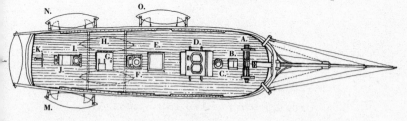

A. windlass
B. forecastle
   companionway
C. foremast
D. tryworks
E. main hatch

F. mainmast and pumps
G. cookhouse
H. spare whaleboat mounted
   on overhead rack
I. mizzenmast
J. aft companionway

K. wheel
L. spare whaleboat
M. starboard boat
N. aft larboard boat
O. waist boat

PREFACE

February 23, 1821

Like a giant bird of prey, the whaleship moved lazily up the western coast of South America, zigging and zagging across a living sea of oil. For that was the Pacific Ocean in 1821, a vast field of warm-blooded oil deposits known as sperm whales. *How they killed sperm whales*

Harvesting sperm whales—the largest toothed whales in existence—was no easy matter. Six men would set out from the ship in a small boat, row up to their prey, harpoon it, then attempt to stab it to death with a lance. The sixty-ton creature could destroy that boat with a flick of its tail, throwing the men into the cold ocean water, often miles from the ship.

Then came the enormous task of transforming a dead whale into oil: ripping off its blubber, chopping it up, and boiling it into the high-grade oil that lit the streets and lubricated the machines of the Industrial Age. That all of this was conducted on the limitless Pacific Ocean meant that the whalemen of the early nineteenth century were not merely seagoing hunters and factory workers but also explorers, pushing out farther and farther into a scarcely charted wilderness larger than all the earth's landmasses combined.

For more than a century, the headquarters of this global oil business had been a little island called Nantucket, twenty-four miles off the coast of southern New England.

It was a Nantucket whaleship, the *Dauphin*, just a few months into what would be a three-year voyage, that was making her way up the

Chilean coast. And on that February morning in 1821, the lookout saw something unusual—a boat, impossibly small for the open sea, bobbing on the swells. The ship's captain, the thirty-seven-year-old Zimri Coffin, trained his spyglass on the mysterious craft with keen curiosity.

He soon realized that it was a whaleboat—a double-ended and about twenty-five-foot-long boat that the whalers used to row from the ship to catch their prey—but a whaleboat unlike any he had ever seen. The boat's sides had been built up by about half a foot. Two makeshift masts had been rigged, transforming the rowing vessel into a rudimentary sailboat. The sails—stiff with salt and bleached by the sun—had clearly pulled the boat along for many, many miles. Coffin could see no one at the steering oar. He turned to the man at the *Dauphin*'s wheel and ordered, "Hard up the helm."

Under Coffin's watchful eye, the helmsman brought the ship as close as possible to the mysterious craft. Even though their momentum quickly swept them past it, the brief seconds during which the ship loomed over the open boat presented a sight that would stay with the crew the rest of their lives.

First they saw bones—human bones—littering the floorboards, as if the whaleboat were the seagoing lair of a ferocious, man-eating beast. Then they saw the two men. They were curled up in opposite ends of the boat, their skin covered with sores, their eyes bulging from the hollows of their skulls, their beards caked with salt and blood.

Instead of greeting their rescuers with smiles of relief, the survivors—too delirious with thirst and hunger to speak—were disturbed, even frightened. They jealously clutched handfuls of gnawed-over bones, refusing to give them up, like two starving dogs found trapped in a pit.

Later, once the survivors had been given some food and water (and had finally surrendered the bones), one of them found the strength to

something terrible happens

tell his story. It was a tale made of a whaleman's worst nightmares: of being in a boat far from land with nothing left to eat or drink and—perhaps worst of all—of a whale with the calculating vengeance of a man.

> ➤ ➤ ➤

The sinking of the whaleship *Essex* by an enraged sperm whale was one of the most well-known marine disasters of the nineteenth century. Nearly every child in America read about it in school. It was the event that inspired the climactic scene of Herman Melville's *Moby-Dick*. *Story inspired Moby-Dick*

But the point at which Melville's novel ends—the sinking of the ship—was merely the starting point for the story of the real-life *Essex* disaster. Of the twenty men who escaped the whale-crushed ship, only eight survived. *Eight men survived*

For nearly 180 years, most of what was known about the calamity came from the 128-page *Narrative of the Wreck of the Whaleship* Essex, written by Owen Chase, the ship's first mate, and published with the help of a ghostwriter only nine months after the first mate's rescue.

Then, around 1960, an old notebook was found in the attic of a home in Penn Yan, New York. Not until twenty years later, in 1980, when the notebook reached the hands of the Nantucket whaling expert Edouard Stackpole, was it realized that its original owner, Thomas Nickerson, had been the *Essex*'s cabin boy. Late in life Nickerson owned and ran a boardinghouse on Nantucket. He had been urged to write an account of the disaster by a writer named Leon Lewis, who may have been one of Nickerson's guests. Nickerson sent Lewis the notebook containing his only draft of the narrative in 1876. For whatever reason, Lewis never prepared the manuscript for publication and eventually gave the notebook to a neighbor, who died with it still in his possession. Nickerson's account was finally published as a limited-edition monograph by the Nantucket Historical Association in 1984.

At fourteen, Thomas Nickerson had been the youngest member of the ship's crew, and his account remains that of a wide-eyed child on the verge of manhood, of an orphan (he lost both his parents before he was two) looking for a home. He was seventy-one when he finally put pen to paper, but Thomas Nickerson could look back to that distant time as if it were yesterday, his memories bolstered by information he'd learned in conversations with other survivors. In the account that follows, Chase will get his due, but for the first time his version of events is challenged by that of his cabin boy, whose testimony can now be heard 182 years after the sinking of the *Essex*.

This story includes owen Chase (first mate) account of the story and Thomas Nickerson's account Nickerson was only 14 and the cabin boy. youngest member of the ship.

1

NANTUCKET

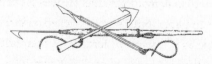

It was, he later remembered, "the most pleasing moment of my life"—the moment he stepped aboard the whaleship *Essex* for the first time. He was fourteen years old, with a broad nose and an open, eager face, and like every other Nantucket boy, he'd been taught to "idolize the form of a ship." The *Essex* might not look like much, stripped of the ropes that made up her rigging and chained to the wharf, but for Thomas Nickerson she was a vessel of opportunity. Finally, after what had seemed an endless wait, Nickerson was going to sea.

The hot July sun beat down on the old, oil-soaked ship until the temperature below was infernal, but Nickerson explored every cranny. "[B]lack and ugly as she was," Nickerson wrote, "I would not have exchanged her for a palace."

In July of 1819 the *Essex* was one of a fleet of more than seventy Nantucket whaleships that sailed the Pacific and Atlantic oceans. With whale-oil prices steadily climbing and the rest of the world's economy sunk in depression, the village of Nantucket was on its way to becoming one of the richest towns in America.

The community of about seven thousand people lived on a gently sloping hill crowded with houses and topped by windmills and church towers. It resembled, some said, the elegant and established port of Salem—a remarkable compliment for an island more than twenty miles out into the Atlantic, below Cape Cod. But if the town, high on its hill, radiated beauty and peace, the waterfront below bustled with activity.

It was a scene familiar to Thomas Nickerson. The children of Nantucket had long used the waterfront as their playground. They rowed old, abandoned whaleboats up and down the harbor and climbed up into the rigging of the ships. To off-islanders it was clear that these children were a "distinctive class of juveniles, accustomed to consider themselves as predestined mariners. . . . They climbed ratlines like monkeys—little fellows of ten or twelve years—and laid out on the yardarms with the most perfect nonchalance." The *Essex* might be Nickerson's first ship, but he had been preparing for the voyage almost his entire life.

He wasn't going alone. His friends Barzillai Ray, Owen Coffin, and Charles Ramsdell, all between the ages of fifteen and eighteen, were also sailing on the *Essex*. Owen Coffin was the cousin of the *Essex*'s new captain and probably steered his three friends to his kinsman's ship. Nickerson was the youngest of the group.

The *Essex* was old and, at eighty-seven feet long, quite small, but she had a reputation on Nantucket as a lucky ship. Over the last decade and a half, she had done well by her Quaker owners, regularly returning at two-year intervals with enough oil to make them wealthy men. Daniel Russell, her previous captain, had been successful enough over the course of four voyages to be given command of a new and larger ship, the *Aurora*. Russell's promotion allowed the former first mate, George Pollard, Jr., to take over command of the *Essex*, and one of the boatsteerers (or harpooners), Owen Chase, to move up to first mate. Three other crew members were elevated to the rank of boatsteerer. Not only a lucky but apparently a happy vessel, the *Essex* was, according to Nickerson, "on the whole rather a desirable ship than otherwise."

Since Nantucket was, like any seafaring town of the period, a community obsessed with omens and signs, such a reputation counted for much. Still, there was talk among the men on the wharves when earlier that July, as the *Essex* was being repaired and outfitted, a comet appeared in the night sky.

From earliest times, the appearance of a comet was interpreted as a sign that something unusual was about to happen. The *New Bedford Mercury*, the newspaper Nantucketers read for lack of one of their own, commented, "True it is, that the appearance of these eccentric visitors have always preceded some remarkable event."

At the wharves there was much speculation, and not just about the comet. All spring and summer there had been sightings up and down the New England coast of what the *Mercury* described as "an extraordinary sea animal"—a serpent with black, horselike eyes and a fifty-foot body resembling a string of barrels floating on the water. Any sailor, especially if he was young and impressionable like Thomas Nickerson, must have wondered if this was, in fact, the best time to be heading out on a voyage around Cape Horn.

Nantucketers had good reason to be superstitious. Their lives were governed by a force of terrifying unpredictability—the sea. Due to a constantly shifting network of sandbars, or "shoals," including the Nantucket Bar just off the harbor mouth, the simple act of coming to and from the island was a dangerous and sometimes deadly lesson in seamanship. Particularly in winter, when storms were the most violent, wrecks occurred almost weekly. Buried throughout the island were the corpses of seamen who had washed up on its shores. Nantucket, which means "faraway land" in the language of the island's native inhabitants, the Wampanoag, was a mound of sand eroding into an unyielding ocean, and all its residents, even if they had never left the island, were all too aware of the inhumanity of the sea.

➤   ➤   ➤

Thomas Nickerson may have enjoyed his first moments aboard the *Essex*, exploring her dark, hot interior, but the thrill was soon over. For the next three weeks, during the warmest summer anyone could remember, Nickerson and the gradually growing crew of the *Essex* worked to prepare the ship. Even in winter, Nantucket's wharves, topped by a layer of oil-soaked sand, stank to the point that people said you didn't see Nantucket when you first rounded the lighthouse at Brant Point, you smelled it. That July and August the stench rising from the wharf must have been bad enough to gag even a veteran whaleman.

At that time on Nantucket it was standard practice to have the newly signed members of a whaleship's crew help prepare the vessel for the upcoming voyage. Nowhere else in New England was a sailor expected to help prepare his ship. That was what riggers, stevedores, and provisioners were for. But on Nantucket, where the Quaker merchants were famous for their ability to cut costs and increase profits, the sailors were expected to do everything.

Whalemen did not work for wages; they were paid a share, or lay— a predetermined portion of the total take—at the end of the voyage. This meant that whatever work a shipowner could extract from a sailor prior to a voyage was, in essence, free or, to Nickerson's mind, "a donation of . . . labor" on the part of the sailor. A shipowner might advance a seaman some money to help him purchase the clothing and equipment necessary for the voyage, but it was deducted (with interest) from his lay at the conclusion of the voyage.

As cabin boy, Thomas Nickerson had what was known as a very "long" (or small) lay. Although the ship papers from the Essex's 1819 voyage have vanished, we know that Nickerson's predecessor, the cabin boy Joseph Underwood of Salem, received a 1/198 lay for the previous voyage. Given that the Essex's cargo of 1,200 barrels of sperm oil sold for about $26,500, Underwood was paid, once the expenses of the voyage were deducted from the gross and his personal expenses were deducted from his own portion, a grand total of about $150 for two years' work. Although this was a pitiful wage, the cabin boy had been provided with room and board for two years and now had the experience to begin a career as a whaleman.

By the end of July, the *Essex*'s upperworks—just about everything at deck level and above—had been completely rebuilt, including a new layer of pine decking and a cookhouse. At some point—probably before Nickerson joined the crew—the *Essex* was laid over on her side for coppering. Immense block-and-tackle systems (a series of pulleys designed for hoisting and hauling) were strung from the ship's masts to the wharf to pull the ship onto her side. The exposed bottom was then covered with copper to protect the ship from marine growth, which could make her four-inch-thick oak hull soft and porous.

At twenty years of age, the *Essex* was reaching the point when many vessels began to exhibit serious structural deterioration. Whale oil seems to have acted as a preservative, providing most whaleships with lives much longer than that of a typical merchant vessel. Still, there were limits. Rot, teredo worms, and a condition called iron sickness, in which the ship's rusted iron fastenings weakened the oak, were all potential problems.

The ever-lengthening voyages around Cape Horn were another concern. "The ship[s] being so long at sea without much repairs," the Quaker merchant Obed Macy wrote in his journal, "must shorten the durations of the ships [by] many years." Indeed, the *Essex* had undergone several days of repairs in South America during her previous voyage. She was an old ship caught up in a new era of whaling, and no one knew how much longer she would last.

Owners were always reluctant to invest any more money in the repair of a ship than was absolutely necessary. While they had no choice but to rebuild the *Essex*'s upperworks, there could well have been suspicious areas below the waterline that they chose to address at a later time, if not ignore. That summer, the *Essex*'s principal owners, Gideon Folger and Sons, were awaiting delivery of a new, much larger whaleship, the *Aurora*. This was not the year to spend more money on a tired old vessel like the *Essex*.

➤   ➤ ➤

Many of Nantucket's whalemen were Quakers, which meant that they were against all armed conflict when it came to the human race. When it came to whales, however, their beliefs were very different. They felt that God had made it their duty to hunt and kill the sperm whale to provide the world with light and to support their families.

While the whalemen pursued their prey throughout the oceans of the world, the Quaker whaling merchants back on Nantucket did everything they could to make as much money as possible, pursuing profits with a lethal enthusiasm.

Gideon Folger and Paul Macy, two major shareholders in the *Essex*, were prominent members of the island's Quaker upper class. Yet, according to Nickerson, Macy, in charge of outfitting the *Essex* that summer of 1819, attempted to cut costs by severely underprovisioning the ship. This was a typical way for shipowners to increase their profits. While it would be unfair to point to Paul Macy as responsible, even in part, for the grief that eventually awaited the men of the *Essex*, the first step toward that future began with Macy's decision to save a little money in beef and hardtack.

Between July 4 and July 23, ten whaleships left the island, most heading out in pairs. The wharves were busy with laborers long into the night, all caught up in the disciplined frenzy of preparing whaleships for sea. But Gideon Folger, Paul Macy, and the *Essex*'s captain, George Pollard, knew that all the preparations would be in vain if they couldn't find a crew of twenty-one men.

Since there were only so many Nantucketers to go around, shipowners relied on off-islanders with no previous sailing experience, known as "green hands," to man their vessels. Many came from nearby Cape Cod and cities up and down the East Coast.

Green hands were typically subjected to what one man remembered as "a sort of examination" by both the shipowner and the captain. Recalled another, "We were catechized, in brief, concerning our nativity and previous occupation, and the build and physical points of each were looked to, not forgetting the eyes, for a sharp-sighted man was a jewel in the estimation of the genuine whaling captain." Some green hands were so naive and poorly educated that they insisted on the longest lay possible, mistakenly thinking that the higher number meant higher pay. The owners were all too willing to grant their wishes.

Whaling captains competed with one another for men. But, as with everything on Nantucket, there were specific rules everyone had to follow. Since first-time captains were expected to defer to all others, the only men available to Captain Pollard of the *Essex* would have been those in whom other captains had no interest. By the end of July, Pollard and the owners were still short by more than half a dozen men.

➤   ➤   ➤

On August 4, Obed Macy stopped by the Marine Insurance Company at the corner of Main and Federal streets to look at the thermometer mounted on its shingled exterior. In his journal he recorded, "93 degrees and very little wind, which has rendered it almost insupportable to be exposed to the rays of the sun."

The next day, August 5, the fully rigged *Essex* was floated over the Nantucket Bar into deep water. Now the loading could begin in earnest, and a series of smaller boats called lighters began ferrying goods from the wharf to the ship. First to be stowed were the ground-tier casks—large, iron-hooped barrels each capable of holding 268 gallons of whale oil. They were filled with seawater to keep them swollen and tight. On top of these were stowed casks of various sizes filled with freshwater. Firewood took up a great deal of space, as did the thousands of shooks, or packed bundles of staves, which would be used by the ship's cooper, or barrel maker, to create more oil casks. On top of that was enough food, all stored in casks, to last two and a half years. If the men were fed the same amount as merchant seamen (which is perhaps assuming too much when it came to a Nantucket whaler), the *Essex* would have contained at least fourteen tons of meat (salt beef and pork), more than eight tons of bread, and thousands of gallons of freshwater. Then there were massive amounts of whaling equipment (harpoons, lances, etc.), as well as clothing, maps, sails (including at least one spare set), navigational instruments, medicine, rum, gin, lumber, and so on. In addition to the three newly painted whaleboats that were suspended from the ship's side by small cranes called "davits," there were at least two spare boats: one stored upside down on a rack over the deck, another mounted over the back of the ship on the thick, multipurpose rods of wood known as spars.

By the time the men were done loading the *Essex* six days later— their labors briefly interrupted by a tremendous shower of rain duly noted by Obed Macy on August 9—the ship was almost as heavily laden as it would be with whale oil on her return to Nantucket. Explained one Nantucketer, "[T]he gradual consumption of provisions and stores keeps pace with the gradual accumulation of oil . . . , and a whaleship is always full, or nearly so, all the voyage."

Something, however, was still missing: the men needed to fill the seven empty berths in the *Essex*'s forecastle. At some point, Gideon Folger put out the call to an agent in Boston for as many black sailors as the agent could find.

➤   ➤   ➤

Although he wasn't black, Addison Pratt came to Nantucket under circumstances similar to the ones that brought seven African Americans to the island and to service on the *Essex*. In 1820,

Pratt found himself in Boston, looking for a ship:

> *I soon commenced hunting for a voyage, but it was dull times with commerce as seamen's wages were but ten dollars per month, and there were more sailors than ships in port, and I found it dull times for green hands. But after looking around for a few days I heard there were hands wanted to go on a whaling voyage to the Pacific Ocean. I made no delay, but hastened to the office and put down my name and received twelve dollars of advance money, which I laid out in sea clothes. . . . Six more hands were shipped for the same vessel, and we were all sent on board of a packet bound to Nantucket.*

As Pratt's account suggests, a whaling voyage was the lowest rung on the maritime ladder for a seaman. Nantucketers like Thomas Nickerson and his friends might look to their first voyage as a necessary step in the beginning of a long and profitable career. But for the men who were typically rounded up by shipping agents in cities such as Boston, it was a different story. Instead of the beginning of something, shipping out on a whaling voyage was often a last and desperate resort.

The seven black sailors who agreed to sign on for a voyage aboard the *Essex*—Samuel Reed, Richard Peterson, Lawson Thomas, Charles Shorter, Isaiah Sheppard, William Bond, and Henry DeWitt—had even fewer choices than Addison Pratt would in 1820. None of their names appear in Boston or New York directories from this period, indicating that they were not landowners. Whether or not they called Boston home, most of them had probably spent more than a few nights in the boardinghouses in the waterfront area of the North End of the city—a place notorious as a gathering place for seamen, black and white, looking for a berth.

As they boarded the packet for Nantucket, the seven African

Americans knew at least one thing: they might not be paid well for their time aboard a Nantucket whaler, but they were assured of being paid no less than a white person with the same qualifications. Since the time when Native Americans had made up the majority of Nantucket's labor force, the island's shipowners had always paid men according to their rank, not their color. Some of this had to do with the Quakers' antislavery leanings, but much of it also had to do with the harsh realities of shipboard life. In a tight spot, a captain didn't care if a seaman was white or black; he just wanted to know he could count on the man to complete his appointed task. Still, black sailors who were delivered to the island as green hands were never regarded as equals by Nantucketers.

➤   ➤   ➤

By the evening of Wednesday, August 11, all except for Captain Pollard were safely aboard the *Essex*. Anchored beside her, just off the Nantucket Bar, was another whaleship, the *Chili*. Commanded by Absalom Coffin, the *Chili* was also to leave the following day. It was an opportunity for what whalemen referred to as a "gam"—a visit between two ships' crews. Without the captains to inhibit the revelry, they may have seized this chance for a final, uproarious fling before the grinding discipline of shipboard life took control of their lives.

At some point that evening, Thomas Nickerson made his way down to his bunk and its mattress full of mildewed corn husks. As he faded off to sleep on the gently rocking ship, he surely felt what one young whaleman described as a great, almost overwhelming "pride in my floating home."

That night he was probably unaware of the latest bit of gossip circulating through town—of the strange goings-on out on the Commons. Swarms of grasshoppers had begun to appear in the turnip fields. "[T]he whole face of the earth has been spotted with them . . . ," Obed Macy would write. "[N]o person living ever knew them so numerous." A comet in July and now a plague of locusts?

As it turned out, things would end up badly for the two ships anchored off the Nantucket Bar on the evening of August 11, 1819. The *Chili* would not return for another three and a half years, and then with only five hundred barrels of sperm oil, about a quarter of what was needed to fill a ship her size. For Captain Coffin and his men, it would be a disastrous voyage.

But nothing could compare to what fate had in store for the twenty-one men of the *Essex*.

Captain
George Pollard.
1st time Captain *28 yrs. old.*

2

KNOCKDOWN

On the morning of Thursday, August 12, 1819, a harbor vessel delivered Captain George Pollard, Jr., to the *Essex*. At twenty-eight, Pollard was a young, but not spectacularly young, first-time captain. Over the last four years he had spent all but seven months aboard the *Essex*, as second mate and then first mate. Except for her former captain, Daniel Russell, no one knew this ship better than George Pollard.

Pollard carried a letter from the *Essex*'s principal owners telling him exactly what was expected of him. His predecessor, Daniel Russell, had received a similar letter prior to an earlier voyage. It had read:

> *Respected Friend,*
>
> *As thou art master of the Ship Essex now lying without the bar at anchor, our orders are, that thou shouldst proceed to sea the first fair wind and proceed for the Pacifick Ocean, and endeavour to obtain a load of Sperm Oil and when accomplished to make the best dispatch for this place. Thou art forbidden to hold any illicit trade. Thou art forbidden to carry on thyself or to suffer any person belonging to the ship Essex to carry on any trade except it should be necessary for the preservation of the ship Essex or her crew: wishing thee a short and prosperous voyage, with a full portion of happiness we remain thy friends.*
>
> *In behalf of the owners of the ship Essex,*
>
> owners of the ship *Gideon Folger, Paul Macy*

Pollard felt the full weight of the owners' expectations. But he was *pollard's wife*

thinking not only about the voyage ahead but also about what he was leaving behind. Just two months before, he and nineteen-year-old Mary Riddell had been married in the Second Congregational Church, of which Mary's father, a well-to-do merchant, was a deacon.

As he scrambled up the *Essex*'s side, Captain Pollard knew that the entire town was watching him and his men. All summer, ships had been leaving the island, sometimes as many as four or five a week, but with the departure of the *Essex* and the *Chili*, there would be a lull of about a month or so before another whaleship would depart. For the entertainment-starved inhabitants of Nantucket, this would be it for a while. *They are leaving Nantucket, Mass.*

Leaving the island was difficult aboard any whaleship, since most of the crew had no idea of what they were doing. It could be an agony of embarrassment for a captain, as the green hands bumbled their *new sailors/not experienced* way around the deck. The whole affair was carried out in the knowledge that the town's old salts and, of course, the owners were watching and criticizing from the shade of the windmills up on Mill Hill.

With, perhaps, a nervous glance toward town, Captain George Pollard gave the order to prepare the ship for weighing the anchors. First mate Owen Chase was stationed in the forward part of the deck. It was his duty to implement Pollard's orders, and he shouted at the men as if every hesitation or mistake on their part were a personal insult.

Pollard and Chase had been together aboard the *Essex* since 1815, when Chase, at eighteen, had signed on as a common sailor. Chase had moved quickly through the ranks. By the next voyage he was a boatsteerer, and now, at only twenty-two, he was the first mate. (Matthew *Owen Chase = 22 yrs. old* Joy, the *Essex*'s second mate, was four years older than Chase.) If all went well during this voyage, Chase would have a good chance of becoming a captain before he was twenty-five.

At five feet ten, Chase was tall for the early nineteenth century; he towered over Captain Pollard, a small man with a tendency toward

[handwritten: Pollard is short and heavy]

stoutness. While Pollard's father was also a captain, Chase's father was a farmer. Perhaps because his father was a farmer on an island where seagoing men got all the glory, Chase was fired with more than the usual amount of ambition and, as he started his third voyage, he made no secret of his impatience to become a captain. "Two voyages are generally considered sufficient to qualify an active and intelligent young man for command," he would write, "in which time, he learns from experience, and the examples which are set him, all that is necessary to be known." He was six years younger than Captain Pollard, but Chase felt he had already mastered everything he needed to know to perform Pollard's job. The first mate's confident attitude would make it difficult for Pollard, a first-time captain just emerging from the long shadow of a respected predecessor, to assert his own style of command.

[handwritten margin notes: "wants to be a Captain"; "younger than Captain Pollard"; "Chase is 6 years younger than Captain Pollard"; "Nickerson is a cabin boy had the function to sweep"]

Nickerson and his Nantucket friends may have thought they knew Chase prior to their departure, but they now realized that, as another young Nantucketer had discovered, "at sea, things appear different." The mate of a Nantucket whaleship routinely underwent an almost Jekyll-and-Hyde transformation when he left his island home, stepping out of his mild Quaker skin to become an unbending dictator. "You will often hear a Nantucket mother boast that her son 'who is *met* of a ship is a real *spit-fire*,' " William Comstock wrote, "meaning that he is a cruel tyrant, which on that island is considered the very *acme* of human perfection."

As cabin boy, Nickerson had to sweep the decks and coil any stray ropes. When he paused for a few seconds to watch his beloved island fade from view behind them, he was accosted by the first mate, who in addition to cuffing him about the ears, snarled, "You boy, Tom, bring back your broom here and sweep clean. The next time I have to speak to you, your hide shall pay for it, my lad!"

And so Nickerson saw Owen Chase change from a perfectly reasonable young man with a new wife named Peggy to a bully who had no qualms about using force to obtain obedience and who swore in a manner that shocked these boys who had been brought up, for the most part, by their mothers and grandmothers. "[A]llthough but a few hours before I had been so eager to go [on] this voyage," Nickerson remembered, "there [now] seemed a sudden gloom to spread over me. A not very pleasing prospect [was] truly before me, that of a long voyage and a hard overseer. This to a boy of my years who had never been used to hear such language or threats before."

It was more than a realization that the whaling life might be harsher than he had been led to believe. Now that the island had slipped over the horizon, Nickerson began to understand, as only an adolescent on the verge of adulthood can understand, that the carefree days of childhood were gone forever: "Then it was that I, for the first time, realized that I was alone upon a wide and an unfeeling world . . . without one relative or friend to bestow one kind word upon me." Not till then did Nickerson begin to appreciate "the full sacrifice that I had made."

➤   ➤   ➤

That evening the men were divided into two shifts, or watches. With the exception of the "idlers"—those such as the cook, steward, and cooper, who worked in the day and slept at night—all the men served alternating four-hour shifts on deck. Like children picking teams on a playground, the mate and second mate took turns choosing the men who would serve in their watches. "[T]he first step taken by the officers," said William Comstock, "is, to discover who are natives of the island, and who are strangers." Once the Nantucketers had all been picked (with Nickerson taken by Chase), the mates chose among the Cape Codders and the blacks.

Next came the choice of oarsmen for the whaleboats, a contest that involved both mates and also Captain Pollard, who headed up his own boat. Since these were the men with whom a mate or a captain was going into battle, he took the selection of the whaleboat crew very

Had been eager for this trip but suddenly felt gloom over himself

seriously. "[T]here was much competition among the officers," a whaleman remembered, "and evidently some anxiety, with a little ill-concealed jealousy of feeling."

Once again, each officer attempted to man his boat with as many fellow Nantucketers as he could. Nickerson found himself on Chase's boat, with the Nantucketer Benjamin Lawrence as a boatsteerer. Nickerson's friend (and the captain's cousin) Owen Coffin was assigned to Pollard's boat along with several other Nantucketers. Matthew Joy, who as second mate was the lowest-ranking officer, was left without a single islander on his boat. The three remaining men not chosen as oarsmen became the Essex's shipkeepers. It was their duty to handle the Essex when whales were being hunted.

The first day of a whaling voyage included yet another ritual—the captain's speech to the crew. The tradition was said to date back to when Noah first closed the doors of the ark, and was the way the captain officially introduced himself. It was a performance that all aboard the ship—officers and green hands alike—attended with great interest.

As soon as Pollard began to speak, Nickerson was impressed by the difference between the captain and the first mate. Instead of shouting and cursing at the men, Pollard spoke "without overbearing display or ungentleman-like language." He simply stated that the success of the voyage would depend on the crew and that the officers should be strictly obeyed. Any sailor who willfully disregarded an order, Pollard told them, would have to answer not just to the officers but to him. He then dismissed the men with the words "Set the watch, Mr. Chase."

The men of the Essex ate and slept in three different areas: the captain's and mates' cabins, in the aft or rear portion of the ship; steerage, where the boatsteerers and young Nantucketers lived, just forward of the officers; and the forecastle—the cramped, poorly lit quarters in the extreme forward part of the vessel, separated from steerage by

Cross-section of the Whaleship *Essex*

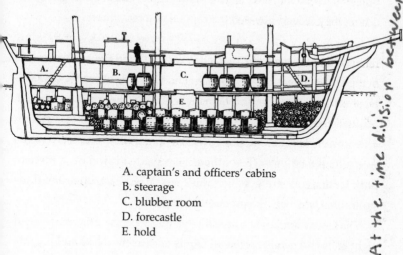

A. captain's and officers' cabins
B. steerage
C. blubber room
D. forecastle
E. hold

At the time division between Whites and Blacks Racism.

the blubber room, where the oil was stored. The divide between the forecastle and the other living quarters was not just physical but also racial. Reflecting the prejudices typical of a Nantucket whaleman, Thomas Nickerson considered himself "fortunate indeed to escape being so closely penned up with so large a number of blacks" in the *Essex*'s forecastle.

But the forecastle had its merits. Its isolation (the only way to enter it was from a hatchway in the deck) meant that its occupants could create their own world. When he sailed on a merchant voyage in the 1830s, Richard Henry Dana, the author of *Two Years Before the Mast*, preferred the camaraderie of the forecastle to steerage, where "[y]ou are immediately under the eye of the officers, cannot dance, sing, play, smoke, make a noise, or *growl* [i.e., complain], or take an other sailor's pleasure." In the forecastle the African American sailors indulged in the ancient seafaring tradition of "yarning"—swapping stories about passages, shipmates, and wrecks, along with other tales of the sea.

They danced and sang songs, often accompanied by a fiddle; they prayed to their God; and, in keeping with yet another oceangoing tradition, they second-guessed the captain and his officers.

➤　➤　➤

By the following morning, many of the green hands found themselves in the throes of seasickness, "rolling and tumbling about the decks almost ready . . . to die or be cast in to the sea," Nickerson remembered. Nantucketers had what they considered a surefire cure for seasickness, a treatment that more delicate mortals might have considered even worse than the illness. The sufferer was made to swallow a piece of pork fat tied to a string, which was then pulled back up again. If the symptoms returned, the process was repeated.

Chase was not about to coddle his queasy crew. That morning at eight bells sharp, he ordered all hands to clear the decks and prepare the ship for whaling. Even though the whale population in the waters to the southeast of the island along the edges of the Gulf Stream had been greatly diminished over the years, it was still quite possible to come across what Nantucketers called a shoal of sperm whales. Woe to the crew that was not ready when a whale was sighted.

But for a whale to be sighted, a lookout had to be positioned aloft at the top of the mast—not a pleasing prospect for a crew of seasick green hands. Every man was expected to climb to the head of the mainmast and spend two hours in search of whales. Some of the men were so weak from vomiting that they doubted they had the strength to hold on to the mast for two hours. One of them, Nickerson said, even went so far as to protest that it was "altogether absurd and unreasonable" to expect them to look for whales, and that he, for one, "should not go, and he hoped the captain would not expect it of him."

The fact that this unnamed sailor specifically mentioned the captain instead of the first mate suggests that he was Pollard's cousin, seventeen-year-old Owen Coffin. Miserable and genuinely fearful for his life, Coffin may have made a desperate, ill-advised appeal to his kinsman for a reprieve from the first mate's discipline. But it was futile. According to Nickerson, whose narrative is not without irony, there followed a few "soft words" from the officers, along with "some little challenging of their spirits," and it wasn't long before all the green hands had taken a turn at the masthead.

>   >   >

Like a skier crossing the face of a mountain, a Nantucket whaleship took an indirect route toward Cape Horn, a course determined by the prevailing winds of the Atlantic Ocean. First, pushed by breezes from the west called "westerlies," the ship sailed south and east toward Europe and Africa. There she picked up winds called the northeast trades, which blew her back east across the ocean again, in the direction of South America. After crossing the equator in an often windless region known as the doldrums, she worked her way south and west through the southeast trades into an area of variable winds. Then she encountered the band of westerlies that could make rounding the Horn so difficult.

On the first leg of this southern slide down the Atlantic, there were stops for provisions at the Azores and Cape Verde Islands, where vegetables and livestock could be purchased for much less than they cost on Nantucket. These stops also gave the whalemen the opportunity to ship back any oil they might have obtained during their cruise across the Atlantic.

On August 15, three days out of Nantucket, the *Essex* was making good time toward the Azores, with the wind out of the southwest, coming directly over her starboard beam, or right side. Having left Nantucket late in the season, the officers hoped to make up lost time.

The *Essex* was moving well, probably at six to eight knots. The lookout spotted a ship ahead. Pollard ordered the helmsman to steer for her, and soon the *Essex* had caught up to what proved to be the whaleship *Midas*, five days out of New Bedford. Captain Pollard and the captain of the *Midas* exchanged shouted greetings, and the *Essex* was soon pulling ahead, her entire crew undoubtedly enjoying the fact that their ship had proved to be what Nickerson called "the fastest sailor of the two."

Later that day, the weather began to deteriorate. Clouds moved into the sky, and it grew suspiciously dark to the southwest. "The sea became very rough," Nickerson remembered, "which caused the ship to roll and tumble heavily." A storm seemed imminent, but the *Essex* "continued to carry a press of sail throughout the night and [the officers] had no cause to disturb the hands except for their respective watches."

Many considerations, both nautical and psychological, went into a decision to reduce the number of sails—a process known as "shortening sail." When the wind built to the point that the ship was tipping too far over, it became time to fold up, or furl, some of the sails. No captain wanted to be needlessly timid, yet taking unnecessary risks, especially at the beginning of a voyage that might last as long as three years, was unwise. At some point the conditions became so rough that Pollard elected to take in some of the sails yet to leave flying the main topgallant and also the studding sails, usually the first sails taken down in worsening weather. Pollard may have wanted to see how the *Essex* performed when pushed to the limit. They sailed on, refusing to back down.

‣   ‣   ‣

According to Chase, they could see it coming: a large black cloud rushing toward them from the southwest. Now was surely the time to shorten sail. But once again they waited, deciding the cloud was an inconsequential gust. They would ride it out. As Chase would later admit, they "miscalculated altogether as to the strength and violence of it."

In delaying, even for a second, shortening sail in the face of an approaching squall, Pollard was now flaunting his disregard of traditional seafaring wisdom. The officers of the British Navy had a maxim: "never to be overtaken unprepared by [a squall], as never to be surprised by an enemy." It was said that the sharper and more defined the storm cloud, the worse the wind; thunder and lightning were also bad signs. When jagged streaks of lightning began to crackle out of the forbidding black sky and thunder boomed, Pollard finally began to issue orders. But it was too late.

In the face of an approaching squall, there were two options: either to point the ship into the oncoming wind, to relieve the pressure on the sails by letting them flap like a flag, or to turn almost 180 degrees in the opposite direction, away from the wind, and let the storm blow the ship with it. Most captains favored turning away from the wind—a strategy that required them to anticipate the arrival of the squall as the crew shortened the upper and aft sails. To attempt to bear away from the wind in the last few seconds before being struck by a squall was to show "a poor appreciation of the squall, or a lack of watchfulness."

This was precisely what happened to the *Essex*. As the squall approached, the man at the wheel was ordered to turn away from the direction of the wind and "run before it." Unfortunately it took time for a ship the size of the *Essex* to respond to her rudder. When the gust slammed into the ship, she had just begun to turn and was sideways to the wind—the worst possible position.

For the green hands, the sound alone was terrifying: the shrieking of the wind across the rigging and then a frenzied flapping of sails and creaking of the masts. The *Essex* began to lurch to the side—slowly at first, the ponderous weight of the ship's keel, not to mention the tons of stores stowed in her hold, refusing at first to yield, but then, as the wind increased, the ship inevitably succumbed to the merciless

[handwritten margin notes: Now around 45 degrees / 11:00 / The ship tilted around 45 degrees]

pressure of the wind and started to turn on its side.

When a ship is tipped over, or heeled, by forty-five degrees or more, her hull might be compared to a fat man on the short end of a lopsided seesaw. No matter how much he weighs, if the end of the seesaw on the other side of the pivot point is long enough, it becomes a lever that will eventually lift him up into the air as the distant tip of the seesaw settles softly to the ground. In the case of the *Essex*, the masts and their wind-pressed sails became levers prying the hull toward the point of no return, forcing it over until the tips of the masts were buried in the water. The *Essex* had been rolled almost ninety degrees onto her side—knocked over on her "beam-ends," in the language of the sea.

Those on deck clung to the nearest fixture, fearful that they might fall down and be trapped in the scuppers—the holes in the sides of the ship that allowed water to run off the deck—now under knee-deep water. Those below deck did their best to shield themselves from objects falling down around them. If he hadn't abandoned it already, the ship's cook was doing his best to scramble out of the cookhouse, the heavy stove and cookware threatening to burst through its frail wooden sides. The two whaleboats on the *Essex*'s port side had disappeared beneath the waves, pressed underwater by the massive weight of the capsized ship. According to Chase, "The whole ship's crew were for a short time thrown into the utmost consternation and confusion."

Yet amid all the chaos there was, at least on deck, a sudden sense of calm. When a ship suffers a knockdown, her hull acts as a barrier against the wind and rain. Even though the ship had been slammed against the water, the men were temporarily sheltered from the howling forces of the wind. Pollard took the opportunity to pull the crew back together. "[T]he cool and undismayed countenance of the captain," Nickerson remembered, "soon brought all to their sober senses."

All of the men are now inside.

The rain poured down and the lightning flashed, and time slowed to a crawl. Suddenly the ship twitched back to life. The men could feel it in their hands and feet and in the pits of their stomachs—an easing of the awful strain. They waited for another gust to slam the ship back down again. But no—the stabilizing weight in the hull (known as ballast) continued to exert its gravitational pull, lifting the three masts until they came clear of the water. As the masts swung into the sky, seawater rushed across the deck and out the scuppers. The *Essex* shuddered to the vertical and was a ship again.

Eventually, the *Essex*'s sails filled, and she was once again making forward progress. Now the crew could do what they should have done before the storm—shorten sail.

As the men aloft wrestled with the canvas, the wind shifted into the northwest and the skies began to brighten. But the mood aboard the *Essex* sank into one of gloom. The ship had been severely damaged. Several sails, including both the main topgallant and the studding sail, had been torn into useless tatters. The cookhouse had been destroyed. The two whaleboats that had been hung off the port side of the ship had been torn from their davits and washed away, along with all their gear. The spare boat on the stern had been crushed by the waves. That left only two workable boats, and a whaleship required a minimum of three, plus two spares. Although the *Essex*'s stern boat could be repaired, they would be without a single spare boat. Captain Pollard stared at the splintered mess and declared that they would be returning to Nantucket for repairs.

His first mate, however, disagreed. Chase urged that they continue on, despite the damage. The chances were good, he insisted, that they would be able to obtain spare whaleboats in the Azores, where they would soon be stopping to procure fresh provisions. Joy sided with his fellow mate. The captain's will was normally the law of the ship. But instead of ignoring his two younger mates, Pollard paused

Pollard said That they are returning to Nantucket.

to consider their arguments. Four days into his first command, Captain Pollard reversed himself. "After some little reflection and a consultation with his officers," Nickerson remembered, "it was deemed prudent to continue on our course and trust to fortune and a kind providence to make up our loss."

The excuse given to the crew was that with the wind now out of the northwest, it would have taken too long to return to Nantucket. Nickerson suspected that Chase and Joy had other motives. Both knew that the men didn't like their rough treatment by the mates. Seeing the knockdown as a bad omen, many of the sailors had become sullen and sour. If they returned to Nantucket, some of the crew would jump ship. Despite the seriousness of the loss of the whaleboats, it was not the time to return to port.

Not surprisingly, given that he was the object of much of the crew's discontent, Chase, in his own account of the accident, never mentions that Pollard originally proposed turning back. As Chase would have it, the knockdown was only a minor inconvenience: "We repaired our damage with little difficulty, and continued on our course." But Nickerson knew differently. Many of the Essex's men were profoundly shaken by the knockdown and wanted to get off the ship. Whenever they passed a homeward-bound vessel, the green hands would lament, in the words of one, "O, how I wish I was onboard with them going home again, for I am heartily sick of these whaling voyages"— even though they had not yet even seen a whale.

coming Towera
Cape Verde islands.

3

FIRST BLOOD

After a provisioning stop in the Azores, which provided plenty of fresh vegetables but no spare whaleboats, the *Essex* headed south toward the Cape Verde Islands. Two weeks later they sighted Boavista Island. In contrast to the Azores' green, abundant hills, the slopes of the Cape Verdes were brown and dry, with no trees to offer relief from the burning subtropical sun. Pollard intended to obtain some hogs at the island of Maio a few miles to the southwest.

The next morning, as they approached the island, Nickerson noticed that Pollard and his mates were strangely excited, speaking to each other as they passed a spyglass back and forth, taking turns studying something on the beach. What Nickerson termed "the cause of their glee" remained a mystery to the rest of the crew until they came close enough to the island to see that a whaleship had been run up onto the beach. Here, perhaps, was a source of some additional whaleboats—something the men of the *Essex* needed much more desperately than pork.

Before Pollard could dispatch one of his own boats to the wreck, a whaleboat was launched from the beach and made its way directly toward the *Essex*. Aboard the boat was the acting American consul, Ferdinand Gardner. He explained that the wrecked whaler was the *Archimedes* of New York. While approaching the harbor she had struck a submerged rock, forcing the captain to run her up onto the beach before she was a total loss. Gardner had purchased the wreck, but he had only a single whaleboat left to sell.

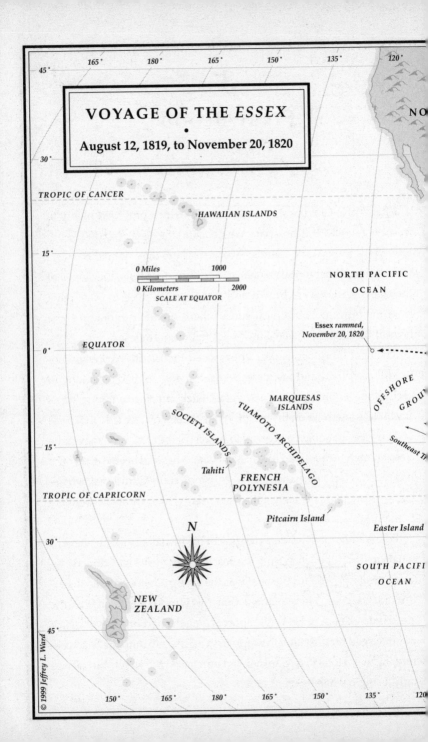

VOYAGE OF THE *ESSEX*

•

August 12, 1819, to November 20, 1820

TROPIC OF CANCER

HAWAIIAN ISLANDS

0 Miles   1000

0 Kilometers   2000

SCALE AT EQUATOR

NORTH PACIFIC

OCEAN

Essex *rammed,*
November 20, 1820

EQUATOR

MARQUESAS
ISLANDS

OFFSHORE

GROUN

SOCIETY ISLANDS

TUAMOTO ARCHIPELAGO

Southeast Tr

Tahiti

FRENCH
POLYNESIA

TROPIC OF CAPRICORN

Pitcairn Island

Easter Island

N

SOUTH PACIFI

OCEAN

NEW
ZEALAND

NO

© 1999 Jeffrey L. Ward

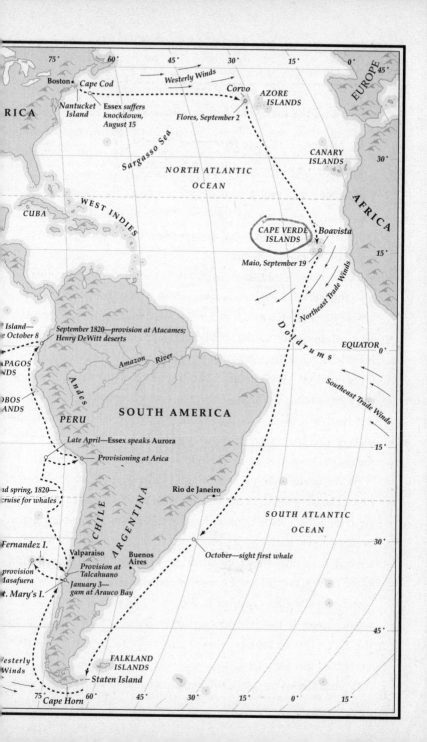

While one was better than nothing, the *Essex* would still be dangerously low on boats. With this latest addition (and an old and leaky addition at that), the *Essex* would now have a total of four whaleboats. That would leave her with only one spare. In a business as dangerous as whaling, boats were so frequently damaged in their encounters with whales that many whaleships were equipped with as many as three spare boats. With a total of only four boats, the crew of the *Essex* would have scant margin for error. That was disturbing. Even the green hands knew that one day their lives could depend on the condition of these fragile boats.

Pollard purchased the whaleboat, then sailed the *Essex* into the cove that served as Maio's harbor, where pointed hills of bone-white salt—procured from salt ponds in the interior of the island—added a sense of desolation to the scene. The *Essex* anchored beside another Nantucket whaleship, the *Atlantic*, which was off-loading more than three hundred barrels of oil for shipment back to the island. Whereas Captain Barzillai Coffin and his crew could boast of the seven or so whales they'd killed since leaving Nantucket on the Fourth of July, the men of the *Essex* were still putting their ship back together after the knockdown in the Gulf Stream and had yet to sight a whale.

White beans were the medium of exchange on Maio, and with a cask of beans aboard, Pollard took a whaleboat into shore to procure some hogs. Nickerson came along. The harbor was without any docks or piers, and in the high surf, bringing a whaleboat into shore was very tricky. Even though they approached the beach at the best possible part of the harbor, Pollard and his men ran into trouble. "Our boat was instantly capsized and overset in the surf," Nickerson recalled, "and thrown upon the beach bottom upwards. The lads did not much mind this for none were hurt, but they were greatly amused to see the captain get so fine a ducking."

Pollard traded one and a half barrels of beans for thirty hogs, whose

Nickerson calls the whales Skeletons.

squeals and grunts and filth turned the deck of the *Essex* into a barn-yard. The impressionable Nickerson was disturbed by the condition of these animals. He called them "almost skeletons," and noted that their bones threatened to pierce through their skin as they walked about the ship.

>　　>　　>

Not until the *Essex* had crossed the equator and reached thirty degrees south latitude—approximately halfway between Rio de Janeiro and Buenos Aires—did the lookout sight the first whale of the voyage. It required sharp eyes to spot a whale's spout: a faint puff of white on the distant horizon lasting only a few seconds. But that was all it took for the lookout to bellow, "There she blows!" or just "B-l-o-o-o-w-s!"

After more than three whaleless months at sea, the officer on deck shouted back in excitement, "Where away?" The lookout's subsequent commentary not only directed the helmsman toward the whales but also worked the crew into an ever-increasing frenzy.

Under the direction of the captain and the mates, the men began to prepare the whaleboats. Tubs of harpoon line were placed into them; the sheaths were taken off the heads of the harpoons, or irons, which were hastily sharpened one last time. "All was life and bustle," remembered one former whaleman.

Once within a mile of the whales, the ship was slowed to a near standstill. The mate climbed into the stern of his whaleboat and the boatsteerer took his position in the bow as the four oarsmen remained on deck and lowered the boat into the water with a pair of block-and-tackle systems known as "the falls." Once the boat was floating in the water beside the ship, the oarsmen—either sliding down the falls or climbing down the side of the ship—joined the mate and boatsteerer. An experienced crew could launch a rigged whaleboat from the davits in under a minute. Once all three whaleboats were in the water, it was up to the three shipkeepers to tend to the *Essex*.

They see a WHALE!!! after three months at sea.

At this early stage in the attack, the mate or captain stood at the steering oar in the stern of the whaleboat while the boatsteerer manned the forward-most, or harpooner's, oar. Aft of the boatsteerer was the bow oarsman. Once the whale had been harpooned, it would be his job to lead the crew in pulling in the whale line. Next was the midships oarsman, who worked the longest and heaviest of the lateral oars—up to eighteen feet long and forty-five pounds. Next was the tub oarsman. He managed the two tubs of whale line. It was his job to wet the line with a small bucketlike container, called a piggin, once the whale was harpooned. This wetting prevented the line from burning from the friction as it ran out around the loggerhead, an upright post mounted on the stern of the boat. Aft of the tub oarsman was the after oarsman. He was usually the lightest of the crew, and it was his job to make sure the whale line didn't tangle as it was hauled back into the boat.

Three of the oars were mounted on the starboard side of the boat and two were on the port side. "Give way all" was the order with which the chase began, telling the men to start rowing together, the after oarsman setting the pace that the other four followed. With all five men pulling at the oars and the mate or captain urging them on, the whaleboat flew like a slender missile over the tops of the waves.

The competition among the boat-crews on a whaleship was always spirited. To be the fastest gave the six men bragging rights over the rest of the ship's crew. The pecking order of the *Essex* was about to be decided.

With nearly a mile between the ship and the whales, the three crews had plenty of space to test their speed. "This trial more than any other during our voyage," Nickerson remembered, "was the subject of much debate and excitement among our crews; for neither was willing to yield the palm to the other."

As the unsuspecting whales moved along at between three and four knots (about four and five miles per hour), the three whaleboats bore down on them at five or six knots (about six or seven miles per hour). Even though all shared in the success of any single boat, no one wanted to be passed by the others; boat-crews were known to foul one another deliberately as they raced side by side behind the giant flukes of a sperm whale.

Nickerson was the after oarsman on Chase's boat, placing him just forward of the first mate at the steering oar. Chase was the only man in the boat who could actually see the whale up ahead. While each mate or captain had his own style, they all coaxed and cajoled their crews with words that evoked the savagery, excitement, and blood-lust associated with pursuing one of the largest mammals on the planet. Adding to the tension was the need to remain as quiet as possible so as not to alarm or "gally" the whale. William Comstock recorded the whispered words of a Nantucket mate:

> *Do for heaven's sake spring. The boat don't move. You're all asleep; see, see! There she lies; skote, skote! I love you, my dear fellows, yes, yes, I do; I'll do anything for you, I'll give you my heart's blood to drink; only take me up to this whale only this time, for this once, pull. Oh, St. Peter, St. Jerome, St. Stephen, St. James, St. John, the devil on two sticks; carry me up; O, let me tickle him, let me feel of his ribs. There, there, go on; O, O, O, most on, most on. Stand up, Starbuck [the harpooner]. Don't hold your iron that way; put one hand over the end of the pole. Now, now, look out. Dart, dart.*

As it turned out, Chase's crew proved the fastest that day, and soon they were within harpooning distance of the whale. Now the attention turned to the boatsteerer, who had just spent more than a mile rowing as hard as he possibly could. His hands were sore, and the muscles in his arms were trembling with exhaustion. All the while he had been forced to keep his back turned to a creature that was now within a few feet, or possibly inches, of him, its tail—more than twelve feet across—working up and down within easy reach of his head. He could hear it—the hollow wet roar of the whale's lungs pumping air in and out of its sixty-ton body.

But for Chase's novice harpooner, the twenty-year-old Benjamin Lawrence, the mate himself was as frightening as any whale. Having been a boatsteerer on the *Essex*'s previous voyage, Chase had definite ideas on how a whale should be harpooned and maintained a continual patter of barely audible, expletive-laced advice. Lawrence tucked the end of his oar handle under the edge of the boat, then braced his leg against the forward deck and took up the harpoon. There it was, the whale's black body, glistening in the sun. The blowhole was on the front left side of the head, and the spout enveloped Lawrence in a foul-smelling mist that stung his skin.

By hurling the harpoon he would transform this gigantic, passive creature into an angry, panicked monster that could easily kill him with a single swipe of that massive tail. Or the whale might turn around and come at them with its tooth-studded jaw opened wide. New boatsteerers had been known to faint dead away when first presented with the terrifying prospect of attaching themselves to an angry sperm whale.

As Lawrence stood at the bow, waves breaking around him, he knew that the mate was analyzing every one of his movements. If he let Chase down now, there would be hell to pay.

"Give it to him!" Chase bawled. "Give it to him!"

Lawrence hadn't moved, when there was a sudden splintering crack and crunch of cedar boards, and he and the other five men were airborne. A second whale had come up from beneath them, giving their boat a tremendous whack with its tail and pitching them into the sky. The entire side of the whaleboat was stove, or smashed in, and the men, some of whom could not swim, clung to the wreck. "I presume the monster was as much frightened as ourselves," Nickerson commented, "for he disappeared almost instantly after a slight flourish of his huge tail." To their amazement, no one was injured.

Pollard and Joy abandoned the hunt and returned to pick up Chase's crew. It was a dispiriting way to end the day, especially since they were once again down a whaleboat, a loss that, in Nickerson's words, "seemed to threaten the destruction of our voyage."

➤   ➤   ➤

Several days after Chase's boat was repaired, the lookout once again sighted whales. The boats were dispatched, a harpoon was hurled—successfully—and the whale line went whizzing out until it finally wrapped tight around the loggerhead, launching the boat and crew on the voyage's first "Nantucket sleigh ride," as it would come to be called.

Merchant seamen spoke derisively about the slow speeds of the average whaleship, but the truth of the matter was that no other sailors in the early nineteenth century experienced the speeds of Nantucket whalemen. And, instead of doing it in the safe confines of a large, three-masted ship, the Nantucketer traveled in a twenty-five-foot boat crammed with half a dozen men, rope, and freshly sharpened harpoons and lances.

The boat rocked from side to side and bounced up and down as the whale dragged it along. When it came to sheer velocity over the water, a Nantucketer—pinned to the side of a whale that was pulling him miles and miles from a whaleship that was already hundreds of miles from land—was the fastest seaman in the world, traveling at fifteen (some claimed as many as twenty) bone-jarring knots.

The harpoon did not kill the whale. It was simply the means by which a whaleboat crew attached itself to its prey. After letting the creature tire itself out—by sounding (or diving) to great depths or simply tearing along the water's surface—the men began to haul themselves, inch by inch, to within stabbing distance of the whale. By this point the boatsteerer and the mate had traded places, a miraculous feat in

Deck Gear—Tools Used for Trying Out a Whale

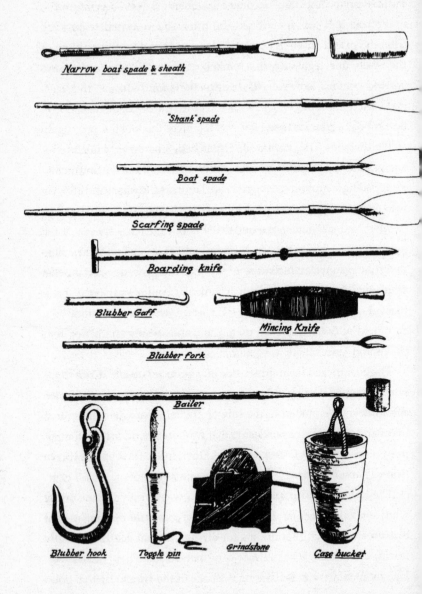

Narrow boat spade & sheath

"Shank" spade

Boat spade

Scarfing spade

Boarding knife

Blubber Gaff

Mincing Knife

Blubber fork

Bailer

Blubber hook

Toggle pin

Grindstone

Case bucket

its own right on a craft as small and tender as a whaleboat. Not only did these two men have to contend with the violent slapping of the boat through the waves—which could be so severe that nails loosened from the planks in the bow and stern—but they had to stay clear of the whale line, quivering like a piano wire down the middle of the boat. Eventually, however, the boatsteerer made it back to the steering oar, and the mate, who was always given the honor of the kill, took up his position in the bow.

If the whale was proving too excited, the mate would injure it by taking up a boat spade and hacking away at the tendons in the tail. Then he'd take up the eleven- to twelve-foot-long killing lance, its petal-shaped blade designed for piercing a whale's vital organs. But finding "the life" of a giant swimming mammal encased in a thick layer of blubber was not easy. Sometimes the mate would be forced to stab it as many as fifteen times, probing for a group of coiled arteries in the vicinity of the lungs with a violent churning motion that soon surrounded the whaleboat in a rushing river of bright red blood.

When the lance finally found its mark, the whale would begin to choke on its own blood, its spout transformed into a fifteen- to twenty-foot geyser of gore that prompted the mate to shout, "Chimney's afire!" As the blood rained down on them, the men took up the oars and backed furiously away, then paused to watch as the whale went into what was known as its flurry. Beating the water with its tail, snapping at the air with its jaws—even as it regurgitated large chunks of fish and squid—the creature began to swim in an ever-tightening circle. Then, just as abruptly as the attack had begun with the first thrust of the harpoon, it ended. The whale fell motionless and silent, a giant black corpse floating fin-up in a slick of its own blood and vomit.

➤   ➤   ➤

The dead whale was usually towed back to the ship headfirst. Even with all five men rowing—the mate at the steering oar sometimes lending a hand to the after oarsman—a boat towing a whale could go no faster than one mile per hour. It was dark by the time Chase and his men reached the ship.

Now it was time to butcher the body to get the oil. The crew attached the whale to the *Essex*'s starboard side, with the head toward the stern. Then they lowered the cutting stage—a narrow plank of wood upon which the mates balanced as they cut up the body. Although the stripping of a whale's blubber has been compared to the peeling of an orange, it was a little less refined than that.

First the mates hacked a hole in the whale's side, just above the fin, into which was inserted a giant hook suspended from the mast. Then the immense power of the ship's windlass, a horizontal cylinder used to create mechanical advantage, was brought to bear, heeling the ship over on its side as the block-and-tackle system attached to the hook creaked with strain. Next the mates cut out the start of a five-foot-wide strip of the blubber adjacent to the hook. Pulled by the tackle attached to the windlass, the strip was gradually torn from the whale's carcass, slowly spinning it around, until a twenty-foot-long strip, dripping with blood and oil, was suspended from the rigging. This "blanket piece" was severed from the whale and lowered into the blubber room belowdecks to be cut into more manageable pieces. Back at the corpse, the blubber-ripping continued.

Once the whale had been completely stripped of blubber, it was decapitated. A sperm whale's head accounts for close to a third of its length. The upper part of the head contains the case, a cavity filled with up to five hundred gallons of spermaceti, a clear, high-quality oil that partially solidifies on exposure to air. After the ship's system of blocks and tackles hauled the head up onto the deck, the men cut a hole into the top of the case and used buckets to remove the oil. One or two men might then be ordered to climb into the case to make sure all the spermaceti had been retrieved. Spillage was inevitable, and soon the decks were a slippery mess of oil and blood. Before cutting loose the whale's mutilated corpse, the mates probed its intestinal tract with a lance, searching for an opaque, ash-colored substance called ambergris. Thought to be the result of indigestion or constipation on the part of the whale, ambergris is a fatty substance used to make perfume and was worth more than its weight in gold.

By now, the two immense, four-barreled iron try-pots were full of pieces of blubber. The blubber was chopped into foot-square hunks, then cut through into inch-thick slabs that resembled the fanned pages of a book and were known as bible leaves. A whale's blubber bears no similarity to the fat reserves of land animals. Rather than soft and flabby, it is tough, almost impenetrable, requiring the whalemen to re-sharpen their cutting tools constantly.

Wood was used to start the fires beneath the try-pots, but once the boiling process had begun, the crispy pieces of blubber floating on the surface of the pot—known as scraps or cracklings—were skimmed off and tossed into the fire for fuel. The flames that melted down the whale's blubber were thus fed by the whale itself. While this was a highly efficient use of materials, it produced thick black smoke with an unforgettable stench. "The smell of the burning cracklings is too horribly nauseous for description," remembered one whaleman. "It is as though all the odors in the world were gathered together and being shaken up."

Trying out a whale could take as long as three days. Special try watches were set, lasting between five and six hours, and affording the men little sleep. Experienced whalemen knew enough to sleep in their trying-out clothes (usually an old short-sleeved shirt and a worn pair of woolen drawers), postponing any attempts at cleaning themselves until the casks of oil had been stored in the hold and the ship had been thoroughly scrubbed down. Nickerson and his friends, however, were so revolted by the noisome mixture of oil, blood, and smoke covering their skin and clothes that they changed after every watch. By the time the first whale had been tried out, they had ruined nearly every piece of clothing stored in their sea chests.

This forced them to purchase additional clothing from the ship's slop chest—the nautical equivalent of the company store—at outrageous prices. Nickerson estimated that if the *Essex* ever made it back to Nantucket, he and his fellow green hands would owe the ship's owners close to 90 percent of their total earnings from the voyage. Instead of warning the teenagers about the potential perils of dipping into the slop chest, the ship's officers were content to let them learn the economics of whaling life the hard way. Nickerson's judgment: "This should not have been."

4

INTO THE PACIFIC

One night, not far from the Falkland Islands, the men were up in the rigging, taking in the topsails, when they heard a scream: a sharp, shrill shriek of terror coming from alongside the ship. Someone had apparently fallen overboard.

The officer of the watch was about to give the order to heave to when a second scream was heard. And then, perhaps with a nervous laugh, someone realized that it wasn't a man but a penguin, bobbing beside the ship, piercing the night with its all-too-human cries. Penguins! They must be nearing Antarctica.

The next day the wind vanished, leaving the *Essex* to languish in a complete calm. Seals played about the ship, "plunging and swimming as though they desired our attention," Nickerson remembered. There were several varieties of penguins, along with gulls pinwheeling in the sky—a sure sign that the *Essex* was approaching land.

While the seals and birds may have provided a distraction, morale about the *Essex* had reached its lowest point. So far it had been a slow and unprofitable trip toward Cape Horn. With the knockdown several days out from Nantucket setting the unfortunate tone of the voyage, they had been more than four months at sea and had only a single whale to show for it. If the voyage continued in this fashion, the *Essex* would have to be out a good deal longer than two years if she were to return with a full cargo of oil. With the temperatures dropping and the legendary dangers of the Horn looming ahead of them, tensions aboard the *Essex* were reaching the breaking point.

➤   ➤   ➤

At eight in the morning on November 25, 1819, the lookout cried, "Land ho!" In the distance, what appeared to be an island of rock towered high above the water. Without hesitation, Captain Pollard pronounced it to be Staten Island, off the eastern tip of Cape Horn. The crew was staring at this legendary sphinxlike sight when suddenly it dissolved in the hazy air. It had been nothing but a fog bank.

Soon after watching the mirage island vanish before them, the men of the *Essex* saw something so terrible that they could only hope their eyes were deceiving them once again. But it was all too real: from the southwest a line of ink-black clouds was hurtling in their direction. In an instant the squall slammed into the ship with the force of a cannon shot. In the shrieking darkness, the crew labored to shorten sail. The *Essex* performed surprisingly well in the mountainous seas. "[T]he ship rode over them as buoyantly as a seagull," Nickerson claimed, "without taking onboard one bucket of water."

But now, with the wind out of the southwest, there was the danger of being driven against the jagged rocks of the Horn. The days became weeks as the ship struggled against the wind and waves in near-freezing temperatures. In these high latitudes the light never entirely left the night sky. Without the usual sequence of light and dark, the passage stretched into a dreary, seemingly unending test of a whaleman's sanity.

It took more than a month for the *Essex* to round Cape Horn. Not until January of the new year, 1820, did the lookout sight the island of St. Mary's, a gathering spot for whalers off the coast of Chile. To the south of the island in the bay of Arauco they found several Nantucket vessels, including the *Chili*, the same ship with which they had left the island five months earlier.

The news from the west coast of South America was not good. For most vessels it had been a miserable whaling season. While the scarcity of whales kept up the price of oil back home on Nantucket, these were tough times for whalemen in the Pacific. After driving his crew to fill his ship, the *Independence,* Captain George Swain had returned to Nantucket in November and predicted, "No other ship will ever fill with sperm oil in the South Seas." Historian Obed Macy feared Captain Swain might be right: "Some new place must be found where the whales are more numerous," he told his journal, "or the business will not be worth pursuing." Praying that they might elude these grim forecasts, the crew of the *Essex* headed out to sea.

After several luckless months off the Chilean coast, punctuated by a provisioning stop at Talcahuano, the *Essex* began to meet with some success off Peru. In just two months, Pollard and his men boiled down 450 barrels of oil, the equivalent of about eleven whales. This meant that they were killing, on average, a whale every five days, a pace that soon exhausted the crew.

The weather only added to their labors. High winds and rugged seas made every aspect of whaling twice as hard. Instead of providing a stable platform on which to cut up the blubber and boil the oil, the *Essex* pitched back and forth in the waves. The rough seas made it next to impossible to lower and raise the whaleboats safely. "Our boats were very much injured in hoisting them from the water," Nickerson remembered, "and were on more than one occasion dashed in pieces by the heavy rolling of the ship." The much-abused boats constantly needed repairs.

It was during this busy and exhausting two-month stretch off Peru that the crew of the *Essex* received what was for a whaleman the ultimate motivator: letters from home.

Toward the end of May, the *Essex* spoke, or hailed, the *Aurora,* the brand-new ship fitted out by Gideon Folger and Sons for Daniel Russell, formerly the captain of the *Essex.* The *Aurora* had left Nantucket on the day after Christmas, bringing with her news that was only five months old—a blink of an eye in the time frame of a whaleman. When the *Aurora* left Nantucket, the price of whale oil was at an all-time high; people were still talking about the fire in Rhoda Harris's schoolroom in the black section of town, known as New Guinea; and they were catching codfish (two hundred to a boat) off the Nantucket village of Siasconset.

But of most interest to the men was the pouch of mail, along with several newspapers, that Daniel Russell handed over to Captain Pollard. After the officers had selected their letters, the bag was sent forward to the crew. "It was amusing to watch those of our lads who had been disappointed and found no letters for them," Nickerson recalled. "They would follow us around the decks and whilst we were reading our letters would seat themselves beside us, as though our letters could be of service to them." Not finding out anything about their own families, the unlucky ones sought solace in what Nickerson called "the careless folds of a newspaper." For his part, Nickerson would reread the newspapers so many times that he would soon have their contents memorized.

The meeting between the *Aurora* and the *Essex* provided Pollard with the chance to speak with his former commander, the thirty-four-year-old Daniel Russell. The *Aurora* was a much larger, state-of-the-art ship and would return to Nantucket two years later, full of oil. Later it would be said that when Captain Russell had left the *Essex* to assume command of the *Aurora*, he had taken his old ship's luck with him.

➤   ➤   ➤

One of the topics Pollard and Russell discussed was the recent discovery of a new whaling ground. As if to refute Captain Swain's grim prediction that the Pacific Ocean had been fished out of sperm whales, Captain George Washington Gardner of the *Globe* had headed farther out to sea in 1818 than any other Nantucket whaleship had so far dared to go. More than a thousand miles off the coast of Peru he hit the mother lode, an expanse of ocean full of sperm whales. He returned home to Nantucket in May of 1820 with more than two thousand barrels of oil.

Gardner's discovery became known as the Offshore Ground. During the spring and summer of 1820, it was the talk of the whale fishery. Understanding that whales appeared in the Offshore Ground in November, Pollard decided to make one final provisioning stop in South America, where he'd secure plenty of fruits, vegetables, and water; then, after touching at the Galapagos Islands, where he would pick up a load of giant tortoises (which were prized for their meat), he would head out for this distant section of ocean.

Sometime in September the *Essex* called at Atacames, a little village of approximately three hundred Spaniards and Indians in Ecuador, just north of the equator.

Something happened there that profoundly influenced the morale of the crew. Henry DeWitt, one of the *Essex*'s African American sailors, deserted.

DeWitt's act came as no great surprise. Sailors fled from whaleships all the time. Once a green hand realized how little money he was likely to make at the end of a voyage, he had no incentive to stay on if he had better options. However, the timing of the desertion could not have been worse for Captain Pollard. Since each whaleboat required a six-man crew, this now left only two shipkeepers whenever whales were being hunted. Two men could not safely manage a square-rigged ship the size of the *Essex*. If a storm should kick up, they would find it almost impossible to shorten sail. Yet Pollard, in a hurry to reach the Offshore Ground by November, had no alternative but to set out to sea shorthanded. Down a crew member and a whaleboat, the *Essex* was about to head out farther off the coast of South America than she had ever sailed before.

At Galapagos islands

5

THE ATTACK

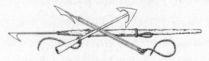

By November 16, 1820, the *Essex* had sailed more than a thousand miles west of the Galapagos Islands. After stopping there to stock up on provisions, including giant turtles, they were following the equator as if it were an invisible lifeline leading the ship ever farther into the largest ocean in the world. Nantucket whalemen were familiar with at least part of the Pacific. Over the last three decades the coast of South America had become their own backyard. They also knew the western edge of the Pacific quite well.

But lying between the island of Timor and the west coast of South America is the Central Pacific, what Owen Chase called "an almost untraversed ocean." All Pollard and his men knew in November of 1820 was that they were at the edge of an unknown world filled with unimaginable dangers. And there was no time for far-flung exploration: it had taken them more than a month to venture out to the Offshore Ground, and it would take at least that to return. They had, at most, only a few months of whaling left before they must think about returning to South America and eventually to Nantucket.

So far, the whales they had sighted in this remote expanse of ocean had proved frustratingly elusive. "Nothing occurred worthy of note during this passage," Nickerson remembered, "with the exception of occasionally chasing a wild shoal of whales to no purpose." Tensions mounted among the *Essex*'s officers. The situation prompted Owen Chase to make an adjustment aboard his whaleboat. When he and his boat-crew did finally approach a whale, on November 16, it was he,

Chase reported, not his boatsteerer, Benjamin Lawrence, who held the harpoon.

This was a radical and, for Lawrence, humiliating turn of events. A mate took over the harpoon only after he had lost all confidence in his boatsteerer's ability to fasten to a whale.

With Chase at the bow and Lawrence relegated to the steering oar, the first mate's boat approached a patch of water where, Chase predicted, a whale would surface. Chase was, in his own words, "standing in the fore part, with the harpoon in my hand, well braced, expecting every instant to catch sight of one of the shoal which we were in, that I might strike." Unfortunately, a whale surfaced directly under their boat, hurling Chase and his crew into the air. Just as had occurred after their first attempt at killing a whale, off the Falkland Islands, Chase and his men found themselves clinging to a wrecked whaleboat.

Given the shortage of spare boats aboard the *Essex*, caution on the part of the officers might have been expected. But caution, at least when it came to pursuing whales, was not part of the first mate's personality. Taking to heart the old adage "A dead whale or a stove boat," Chase loved the risk and danger of whaling. "The profession is one of great ambition," he would boast in his narrative, "and full of honorable excitement: a tame man is never known amongst them."

➤   ➤   ➤

Four days later, on November 20, more than 1,500 nautical miles west of the Galapagos and just 40 miles south of the equator, the lookout saw spouts. It was about eight in the morning of a bright clear day. Only a slight breeze was blowing. It was a perfect day for killing whales.

Once they had sailed to within a half mile of the shoal, the two shipkeepers headed the *Essex* into the wind, and the three boats were lowered. The whales, unaware that they were being pursued, sounded beneath the waves.

Chase directed his men to row to a specific spot, where they waited "in anxious expectation," scanning the water for the dark shape of a surfacing sperm whale. Once again, Chase tells us, he was the one with the harpoon, and sure enough, a small whale emerged just ahead of them and spouted. The first mate readied to hurl the harpoon and, for the second time in as many days of whaling, ran into trouble.

Chase had ordered Lawrence, the ex-harpooner, to steer the boat in close to the whale. Lawrence did so, so close that as soon as the harpoon sliced into it, the panicked animal whacked the already battered craft with its tail, opening up a hole in the boat's side. As water poured in, Chase cut the harpoon line with a hatchet and ordered the men to stuff their coats and shirts into the jagged opening. While one man bailed, they rowed back to the ship. Then they pulled the boat up onto the *Essex*'s deck.

By this time, both Pollard's and Joy's crews had fastened to whales. Angered that he had once again been knocked out of the hunt, Chase began working on his damaged boat with a fury, hoping to get the craft back in the water while whales were still to be taken. Although he could have outfitted and lowered the extra boat (the one they had bargained for in the Cape Verde Islands, now lashed to the rack over the quarterdeck), Chase felt it would be faster to repair the damaged boat temporarily by stretching some canvas across the hole. As he nailed the edges of the canvas to the boat, his after oarsman, Thomas Nickerson—all of fifteen years old—took over the helm of the *Essex* and steered the ship toward Pollard and Joy, whose whales had dragged them several miles away. It was then that Nickerson saw something off the port bow.

It was a whale—a huge sperm whale, the largest they'd seen so far—a male about eighty-five feet long, they estimated, and approximately eighty tons. It was less than a hundred yards away, so close that they could see that its giant blunt head was etched with scars, and that it was pointed toward the ship. But this whale wasn't just large. It was acting strangely. Instead of fleeing in panic, it was floating quietly on the surface of the water, puffing occasionally through its blowhole, as if it were watching them. After spouting two or three times, the whale dove, then surfaced less than thirty-five yards from the ship.

Even with the whale just a stone's throw from the *Essex*, Chase did not see it as a threat. "His appearance and attitude gave us at first no alarm," he wrote. But suddenly the whale began to move. Its twenty-foot-wide tail pumped up and down. Slowly at first, with a slight side-to-side waggle, it picked up speed until the water crested around its massive barrel-shaped head. It was aimed at the *Essex*'s port side. In an instant, the whale was only a few yards away—"coming down for us," Chase remembered, "with great celerity."

In desperate hopes of avoiding a direct hit, Chase shouted to Nickerson, "Put the helm hard up!" Several other crew members cried out warnings. "Scarcely had the sound of the voices reached my ears," Nickerson remembered, "when it was followed by a tremendous crash." The whale rammed into the forward side of the ship.

The *Essex* shook as if she had struck a rock. Every man was knocked off his feet. Galapagos tortoises went skittering across the deck. "We looked at each other with perfect amazement," Chase recalled, "deprived almost of the power of speech."

As they pulled themselves up off deck, Chase and his men had good reason to be amazed. Never before, in the entire history of the Nantucket whale fishery, had a whale been known to attack a ship. In 1807 the whaleship *Union* had accidentally plowed into a sperm whale at night and sunk, but something very different was happening here.

After the impact, the whale passed underneath the ship, bumping the bottom so hard that it knocked off the false keel—a formidable six-by-twelve-inch timber that formed the backbone of the ship. The whale surfaced at the *Essex*'s starboard side. The creature appeared, Chase remembered, "stunned with the violence of the blow" and floated beside the ship, its tail only a few feet from the stern.

Instinctively, Chase grabbed a lance. All it would take was one perfectly aimed throw and the first mate might slay the whale that had dared to attack a ship. This giant creature would yield more oil than two, maybe even three, normal-sized whales. If Pollard and Joy also proved successful that day, they would be boiling down at least 150 barrels of oil in the next week—more than 10 percent of the *Essex*'s total capacity. They might be heading back to Nantucket in a matter of weeks instead of months.

Chase motioned to stab the bull—still lying side by side with the *Essex*. Then he hesitated. The whale's flukes, he noticed, were dangerously close to the ship's rudder. If provoked, the whale might smash the delicate steering device with its tail. They were too far from land, Chase decided, to risk damaging the rudder.

For the first mate, it was a highly uncharacteristic display of caution. "But could [Chase] have foreseen all that so soon followed," Nickerson wrote, "he would probably have chosen the lesser evil and have saved the ship by killing the whale even at the expense of losing the rudder."

➤   ➤   ➤

A sperm whale is uniquely equipped to survive a head-on collision with a ship. Stretching for a third of its length between the front of the whale's battering-ram-shaped head and its vital organs is an oil-filled cavity perfectly adapted to cushioning the impact of a collision. In less than a minute, this eighty-ton bull was once again showing signs of life.

Snapping out of its daze, the whale swam approximately six hundred yards away. There it began clapping its jaws and thrashing the water with its tail, "as if distracted," Chase wrote, "with rage and fury." The whale then swam back toward the ship, crossing the

Essex's bow at a high rate of speed. Several hundred yards ahead of the ship, the whale stopped and turned in the *Essex*'s direction. Fearful that the ship might be taking on water, Chase had, by this point, ordered the men to rig the pumps. "[W]hile my attention was thus engaged," the first mate remembered, "I was aroused with the cry of a man at the hatchway, 'Here he is—he is making for us again.' " Chase turned and saw a vision of "fury and vengeance" that would haunt him in the long days ahead.

With its huge scarred head halfway out of the water and its tail beating the ocean into a white-water wake more than forty feet across, the whale approached the ship at twice its original speed—at least six knots. Chase, hoping "to cross the line of his approach before he could get up to us, and thus avoid what I knew, if he should strike us again, would prove our inevitable destruction," cried out to Nickerson, "Hard up!" But it was too late for a change of course.

With a tremendous cracking and splintering of oak, the whale struck the ship just beneath the anchor secured at the port bow. This time the men were prepared for the hit. Still, the force of the collision caused the whalemen's heads to snap back on their muscled necks as the ship lurched to a halt on the forehead of the whale. The creature's tail continued to work up and down, pushing the 238-ton ship backward until water surged up over the transom at the aft, or back, part of the ship.

One of the men who had been belowdecks ran up onto the deck, shouting, "The ship is filling with water!" A quick glance down the hatchway revealed that the water was already above the lower deck, where the oil and provisions were stored.

No longer going backward, the *Essex* was now going down. The whale, having crippled its strange adversary, drew away from the shattered timbers of the copper-sheathed hull and swam off, never to be seen again.

➤   ➤   ➤

The ship was sinking bow-first. The forecastle, where the black sailors slept, was the first of the living quarters to flood, the men's sea chests and mattresses floating on the rising tide. Next the water surged aft into the blubber room, then into steerage, where Nickerson and the other Nantucketers slept. Soon even the mates' and captain's cabins were underwater.

As the belowdecks creaked and gurgled, the black steward, William Bond, on his own initiative, returned several times to the rapidly filling cabins to retrieve Pollard's and Chase's trunks and—with great foresight—the navigational equipment. Meanwhile Chase and the rest of the crew cut free the spare whaleboat and carried it to the side of the ship.

The *Essex* began to lean dangerously to port. Bond made one last plunge below. Chase and the others carried the whaleboat to the edge of the deck, now only a few inches above the ocean's surface. When the trunks and other equipment had been loaded aboard, everyone, including Bond, scrambled into the boat, the tottering masts looming above them. They were no more than two boat lengths away when the *Essex*, with an appalling slosh and groan, capsized behind them.

Just at that moment, two miles to leeward, Obed Hendricks, Pollard's boatsteerer, casually glanced over his shoulder. He couldn't believe what he saw. From that distance it looked as if the *Essex* had been hit by a sudden squall, the sails flying in all directions as the ship fell onto her beam-ends.

"Look, look," he cried, "what ails the ship? She is upsetting!"

But when the men turned to look, there was nothing to see. "[A] general cry of horror and despair burst from the lips of every man," Chase wrote, "as their looks were directed for [the ship], in vain, over every part of the ocean." The *Essex* had vanished below the horizon.

The two boat-crews immediately released their whales and began rowing back toward the place the *Essex* should have been—all the time speculating frantically about what had happened to the ship. It never occurred to any of them that, in Nickerson's words, "a whale [had] done the work." Soon enough, they could see the ship's hull "floating upon her side and presenting the appearance of a rock."

As Pollard and Joy approached, the eight men crowded into Chase's boat continued to stare silently at the ship. "[E]very countenance was marked with the paleness of despair," Chase recalled. "Not a word was spoken for several minutes by any of us; all appeared to be bound in a spell of stupid consternation."

From the point at which the whale first attacked, to the escape from the capsizing ship, no more than ten minutes had elapsed. In only a portion of that time, spurred by panic, eight of the crew had launched an unrigged whaleboat from the rack above the quarterdeck, a process that would have normally taken at least ten minutes and required the effort of the entire ship's crew. Now, here they were, with only the clothes on their backs, huddled in the whaleboat. It was not yet ten in the morning.

It was then that Chase fully appreciated what William Bond had done. He had salvaged two compasses, two copies of Nathaniel Bowditch's *New American Practical Navigator*, and two quadrants. Chase later called this equipment "the probable instruments of our salvation. . . . [W]ithout them," he added, "all would have been dark and hopeless."

For his part, Thomas Nickerson was swept by a sense of grief, not for himself, but for the ship. The giant black craft that he had come to know so intimately had been dealt a deathblow. "Here lay our beautiful ship, a floating and dismal wreck," Nickerson lamented, "which but a few minutes before appeared in all her glory, the pride and boast of her captain and officers, and almost idolized by her crew."

Soon the other two whaleboats came within hailing distance. But no one said a word. Pollard's boat was the first to reach them. The men stopped rowing about thirty feet away. Pollard stood at the steering oar, staring at the capsized hulk that had once been his formidable command, unable to speak. He dropped down onto the seat of his whaleboat, so overcome with astonishment, dread, and confusion that Chase "could scarcely recognize his countenance." Finally Pollard asked, "My God, Mr. Chase, what is the matter?"

Chase's reply: "We have been stove by a whale."

➤   ➤   ➤

After listening to the first mate's account of the sinking, Pollard attempted to take command of the dire situation. Their first priority, he announced, was to get as much food and water out of the wreck as possible. To do that, they needed to cut away the masts so that the still partially floating hull could be turned upright. The men climbed onto the ship and began to hack away at the spars and rigging with hatchets from the whaleboats. As noon approached, Captain Pollard shoved off in his boat to take an observation with his quadrant. They were at latitude 0°40' south, longitude 119°0' west, just about as far from land as it was possible to be anywhere on earth.

Forty-five minutes later, the masts had been reduced to twenty-foot stumps and the Essex was floating partly upright again, at a forty-five-degree angle. Although most of the provisions were unreachable in the lower hold, there were two large casks of bread between decks in the waist of the ship. And since the casks were on the Essex's upper side, the men could hope that they were still dry.

Through the holes they chopped into the deck they were able to extract six hundred pounds of hardtack. Elsewhere they broke through the planks to find casks of freshwater—more, in fact, than they could safely hold in their whaleboats. They also scavenged tools and equipment, including two pounds of boat nails, a musket, two pistols, and a small canister of powder. Several Galapagos tortoises swam to the whaleboats from the wreck, as did two skinny hogs. Then it began to blow.

In need of shelter from the mounting wind and waves, yet fearful the *Essex* might at any moment break up and sink like a stone, Pollard ordered that they tie the boats to the ship but leave at least a hundred yards of line between it and themselves. Like a string of ducklings trailing their mother, they spent the night beside the ship.

> ➤   ➤   ➤

The ship shuddered with each wave. Chase lay sleepless in his boat, staring at the wreck and reliving the catastrophe over and over again in his mind. Some of the men slept and others "wasted the night in unavailing murmurs," Chase wrote. Once, he admitted, he found himself breaking into tears.

Part of him was guilt-wracked, knowing that if he had only hurled the lance, it might have all turned out differently. (When it came time to write his own account of the attack, Chase would neglect to mention that he had the chance to lance the whale—an omission Nickerson made sure to correct in his narrative.) But the more Chase thought about it, the more he realized that no one could have expected a whale to attack a ship, and not just once but twice. Instead of acting as a whale was supposed to—as a creature "never before suspected of premeditated violence, and proverbial for its inoffensiveness"—this big bull had been possessed by what Chase finally took to be a very human concern for the other whales. "He came directly from the shoal which we had just before entered," the first mate wrote, "and in which we had struck three of his companions, as if fired with revenge for their sufferings."

As they bobbed in the shelter of the wreck, the men of the *Essex* were of no mind to debate the whale's motives. Their overwhelming question was how twenty men in three boats could get out of this alive.

6

THE PLAN

All night the wind blew out of the southeast. Waves beat against the stricken hull, dislodging spars and casks and splintering timbers. Jagged debris might at any time pierce the frail sides of the three whaleboats tied up to the ship, so each officer posted a man in the bow of his boat and commanded him to keep a sharp lookout for floating objects bearing down on them and to shove those objects aside before they could do damage. It was terrifying duty—straining to see what threat would next emerge from the darkness.

When the sun lit the eastern horizon, the men rose up blinking from the bottoms of the boats, most of them having had little sleep. "[W]e began to think of doing something," Chase recalled, "what, we did not know."

The three boat-crews returned to the wreck, and for most of the morning the men wandered about the wave-washed deck "in a sort of vacant idleness." The officers instructed them to search for any additional provisions that might have floated up from the depths of the hold during the night. Except for a few more Galapagos tortoises, of which they already had as many as could be safely carried in the whaleboats, they found nothing of use.

The obvious next step was to make preparations for leaving the wreck. But this was a prospect that none of the men wanted to contemplate, no matter how "cheerless and desolate" their current circumstances might be. "Our thoughts . . . hung about the ship, wrecked and sunken as she was," Chase remembered, "and we could scarcely discard from our minds the idea of her continuing protection."

Eventually some of the men began stripping the sails off the ship to make sails for the three whaleboats. Luckily Chase's trunk contained the necessary needles and twine, and the men set to work. Others were directed to build masts for the whaleboats from the ship's spars. Once the crew had been given specific tasks to accomplish, the change in morale was swift. Nickerson noticed "more cheerful faces than we dared to expect."

As the men worked—equipping each boat with two short masts, two spritsails, and a small sail up forward known as a jib—a lookout remained posted on the stump of the *Essex*'s foremast, gazing out across the ocean for another ship. At noon, Chase took an observation and determined that the prevailing southeasterly winds and westerly current had driven the *Essex* and her crew almost fifty miles to the northwest of where they'd been the day before—*away* from the distant coast of South America. For the first mate, this troubling information made clear "the necessity of not wasting our time, and of endeavoring to seek some relief wherever God might direct us."

The wind increased throughout the day, making it difficult to work in the whaleboats, especially when waves broke across them, drenching the men. The officers realized that some further modifications were necessary to increase the vessels' seaworthiness. Using rough cedar boards from the wreck, the men built up the sides of each boat by more than half a foot. This simple alteration—done almost as an afterthought—proved crucial. "[T]he boats must otherwise have taken in so much water," Chase wrote, "that all the efforts of twenty such weak, starving men as we afterwards came to be, would not have sufficed to keep [them from swamping]."

It was also now clear that they had to work out some method of shielding their provisions of bread from the salt spray. Each end of the whaleboat contained a cupboardlike space called a cuddy.

Have to take off sails from the big ship

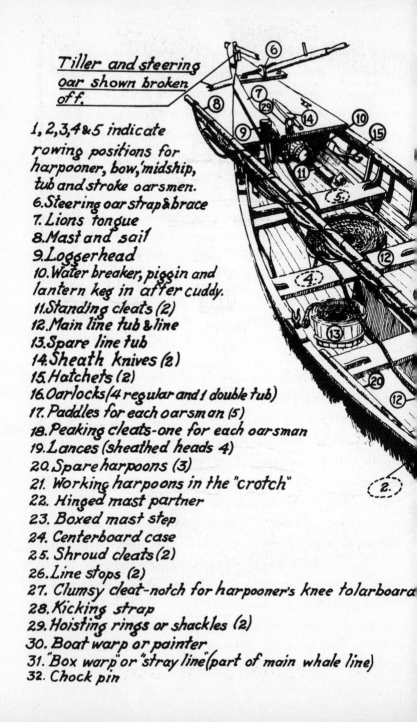

Tiller and steering oar shown broken off.

1, 2, 3, 4 & 5 indicate rowing positions for harpooner, bow, 'midship, tub and stroke oarsmen.
6. Steering oar strap & brace
7. Lions tongue
8. Mast and sail
9. Loggerhead
10. Water breaker, piggin and lantern keg in after cuddy.
11. Standing cleats (2)
12. Main line tub & line
13. Spare line tub
14. Sheath knives (2)
15. Hatchets (2)
16. Oarlocks (4 regular and 1 double tub)
17. Paddles for each oarsman (5)
18. Peaking cleats-one for each oarsman
19. Lances (sheathed heads 4)
20. Spare harpoons (3)
21. Working harpoons in the "crotch"
22. Hinged mast partner
23. Boxed mast step
24. Centerboard case
25. Shroud cleats (2)
26. Line stops (2)
27. Clumsy cleat-notch for harpooner's knee tolarboard
28. Kicking strap
29. Hoisting rings or shackles (2)
30. Boat warp or painter
31. "Box warp" or "stray line" (part of main whale line)
32. Chock pin

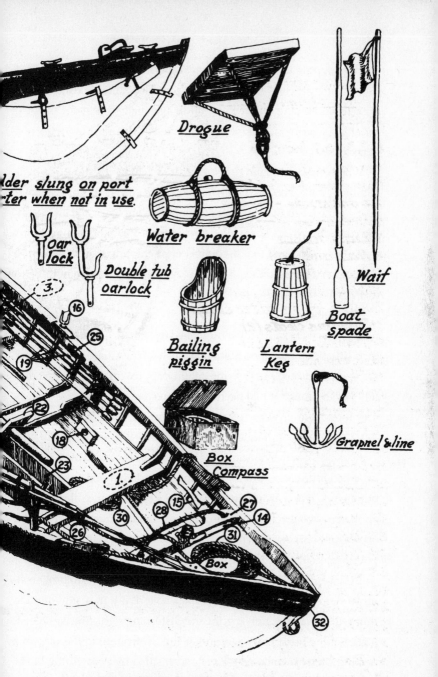

Drogue

lder slung on port
ter when not in use.

oar lock

Double tub oarlock

Water breaker

Bailing piggin

Lantern Keg

Box Compass

Waif

Boat spade

Grapnel & line

Box

Whaleboat & Gear

After wrapping the bread in several layers of canvas, they placed it in the boat's aft cuddy, as far as they could from the waves breaking at the bow. Having it in the aft cuddy also made it easy for the officer at the steering oar to monitor the bread's distribution to the rest of the crew.

When darkness began to come on, they reluctantly put aside their hammers, nails, needles, and twine and once again tied up the whaleboats in the lee of the wreck. It was still blowing hard, and all twenty men dreaded what Chase called "the horrors of another tempestuous night." It wasn't just the discomfort of attempting to sleep in a tiny rocking boat but also the prospect of an entire night with nothing to distract them from their fears.

The same men who had worked so cheerfully at modifying the whaleboats were suddenly bludgeoned by despair. "[T]he miseries of their situation came upon them with such force," Chase remembered, "as to produce spells of extreme debility, approaching almost to fainting." Even though it had been almost two days since their last meal, they found it impossible to eat. Their throats parched by anxiety, they indulged instead in frequent drinks of water.

Chase lay down in the bottom of his boat and began to pray. But this provided little consolation: "Sometimes . . . a light hope would dawn, but then, to feel such an utter dependence on . . . chance alone for aid and rescue, would chase it again from my mind." Chase found himself once again reliving the circumstances that had brought them to this point, especially "the mysterious and mortal attack of the animal."

By seven o'clock the next morning, the ship's deck had broken almost entirely from the hull. Like a whale dying in a slow-motion flurry, the *Essex* was now a grim and disturbing sight. She was bleeding from the burst casks within her hull, surrounding the men in a reeking slick of whale oil—a yellowish slime that coated the boats' sides and slopped over the gunwales with the waves. The boats became slippery and dangerous to move around in. The fluid that only a few days before had been their fortune, their obsession, was now their torment.

Chase decided that something must be done. He rowed over to Pollard and declared that it was time for them to sail "towards the nearest land." The captain stalled, insisting that they scavenge the wreck one last time for provisions they might have overlooked. Only after he had the opportunity for another observation at noon, he said, would he discuss what to do next.

Pollard's noon observation revealed that they had drifted nineteen miles to the north, taking them across the equator during the night. Now, with their sails ready and Pollard's navigational calculations complete, it was time for what Chase termed a "council." So, with his two mates joining him in his whaleboat, Pollard spread out before them their two copies of Bowditch's *Navigator* and its list of the latitudes and longitudes of "Friendly and other Islands in the Pacific Ocean" and began the discussion of what they should do.

Since their sail-equipped whaleboats could travel only *with* the wind, their options were quite limited. Backtracking their way to the Galapagos and beyond that to South America, a trip of more than two thousand miles, meant going against both the southeasterly trade winds and a strong west-flowing current. Pollard deemed it impossible. Sailing to the west, however, was another matter. The closest islands in this direction were the Marquesas, about 1,200 miles away. Unfortunately, the *Essex* men had heard that their native inhabitants had a reputation for cannibalism. The officers agreed that the Marquesas must be avoided.

Several hundred miles to the south of the Marquesas were the islands of the Tuamotu Archipelago. These, too, had a dark and disturbing reputation among American sailors. To the west of the Tuamotus were the Society Islands, about two thousand miles away.

Although he had no trustworthy information to go on, Pollard was under the impression that the Society Islands were a safer option than the Marquesas. With a little luck, these islands might be reached in less than thirty days. There were also the Hawaiian Islands, more than 2,500 miles to the northwest, but Pollard was fearful of the storms that frequented this region of the Pacific in the late fall. He stated his conclusion: they should sail for the Society Islands.

Chase and Joy disagreed. They pointed out that, except for vague rumors, they were "entirely ignorant" of the Society islands. "[I]f [the islands were] inhabited," the first mate wrote, "we presumed they were by savages, from whom we had as much to fear, as from the elements, or even death itself." Nature had already betrayed them once—with the vicious attack on them by the normally benign sperm whale. In the absence of any strong evidence to the contrary, Chase and Joy believed that the people of the Society Islands practiced, like the Marquesans, an even more horrific inversion of the natural order: the eating of human flesh.

Chase and Joy proposed what they felt was a better alternative. Although the easterly slant of the trade winds ruled out sailing directly for the coast of South America, there was another possibility. If they sailed south for about 1,500 miles to latitude 26° south, they would enter a band of variable breezes which they could then ride to Chile or Peru. They figured their boats could cover a degree of latitude—sixty nautical miles—a day. That would put them in the variables in twenty-six days; thirty days later and they would be on the coast of South America. With enough bread and water to last about sixty days, it all seemed—at least to Chase and Joy—very feasible. And besides, somewhere along the way they might be spotted by another whaleship. The two mates lightly described their proposal as "going up the coast."

Just as he had after the knockdown in the Gulf Stream, Pollard succumbed to them. "Not wishing to oppose where there was two against one," Nickerson remembered, "the captain reluctantly yielded to their arguments." When writing of this "fatal error" later, the *Essex*'s cabin boy asked, "How many warm hearts have ceased to beat in consequence of it?"

> ➤ ➤ ➤

Today, the Nantucketers' lack of knowledge of the Pacific, an ocean in which they had been sailing for several decades, seems incredible. Since before the turn of the century, trade ships from the nearby ports of New York, Boston, and Salem had been making frequent stops at not only the Marquesas but also the Hawaiian Islands on their way to China. While rumors of cannibalism in the Marquesas were widespread, there was plenty of readily accessible information to the contrary, including an article that appeared in a local newspaper. Unfortunately, Pollard and his officers appear not to have read the report.

Their ignorance of the Society Islands, in particular Tahiti, is even more extraordinary. Since 1797, there had been a thriving English mission on the island. Tahiti's huge royal mission chapel, 712 feet long and 54 feet wide, was bigger than any Quaker meetinghouse on Nantucket.

The men of the *Essex* were the victims of their particular moment in the history of the whale fishery. The Offshore Ground had been discovered only the year before. In another few years whaleships would go so far from the coast of South America that they would be compelled to provision in the islands of the Central Pacific, making the opening up of the Marquesas and the Society Islands to the west an accomplished fact. But in November 1820, these islands were outside the bounds of what they considered to be reliable knowledge.

Nantucketers were suspicious of anything beyond their immediate experience. Their far-reaching success in whaling was founded not on radical technological advances or bold gambles but on a profound conservatism. Gradually building on the achievements of the generations before them, they had expanded their whaling empire in a most deliberate and painstaking manner. If new information didn't come to them from the lips of another Nantucketer, it was suspect.

By spurning the Society Islands and sailing for South America, the *Essex* officers chose to take their chances with an element they did know well: the sea. "The whaling business is peculiarly an ocean life," Obed Macy wrote. "The sea, to mariners generally, is but a highway over which they travel to foreign markets; but to the whaler it is his field of labor, it is the home of his business." Or, as Melville would write in the "Nantucket" chapter of *Moby-Dick:* "The Nantucketer, he alone resides and rests on the sea; he alone, in Bible language, goes down to it in ships; to and fro ploughing it as his own special plantation. *There* is his home; *there* lies his business, which a Noah's flood would not interrupt, though it overwhelmed all the millions in China."

For these Nantucketers the prospect of a long-distance voyage in twenty-five-foot boats was certainly daunting, but it was a challenge for which they were prepared. Their vessels, after all, were not cumbersome, run-of-the-mill lifeboats; these were whaleboats, high-performance craft that had been designed for the open ocean. Made of light, half-inch-thick cedar planks, a whaleboat possessed the buoyancy required to ride over rather than through the waves.

The perils of whaling had given the Nantucketers a high tolerance for danger and suffering. They had been tossed in the air by the flukes of a whale; they had spent hours clinging to the battered remains of a capsized whaleboat in a cold and choppy sea. "We are so much accustomed to the continual recurrence of such scenes as these," Chase wrote, "that we become familiarized to them, and consequently always feel that confidence and self-possession, which teaches us every expedient in danger, and inures the body, as well as the mind, to fatigue, privation, and peril, in frequent cases exceeding belief." Only

a Nantucketer in November 1820 possessed the necessary combina-
tion of arrogance, ignorance, and fear to shun a beckoning (albeit
unknown) island and choose instead an open-sea voyage of several
thousand miles.

>   >   >

Now that they had devised a plan, it was time to split up the crew
among the three whaleboats. Since Chase's boat was in the worst
shape, his crew remained at just six, while the other boats were obliged
to carry seven men each.

At the beginning of the voyage, the officers' prime consideration
when choosing a man for a boat-crew had been whether or not he
was a Nantucketer. In the aftermath of a disaster, ties of family and
friendship are, if anything, even more strongly felt, and it is apparent
that the Nantucketers' clannishness, now intensified, strongly influenced the makeup of the three crews. So did rank. Of the twenty crew
members, nine were Nantucketers, five were white off-islanders, and
six were African Americans. As captain, Pollard was given the most
Nantucketers—five out of the seven men in his boat. Chase managed
to get two, along with two white Cape Codders and a black. Second
mate Matthew Joy, however, the Essex's most junior officer, found
himself without a single Nantucketer; instead he was given four of the
six blacks.

Feeling personally responsible for the welfare of the young Nantucketers aboard the Essex, Pollard made sure that his boat contained
his eighteen-year-old cousin, Owen Coffin, and Coffin's two boyhood
friends, Charles Ramsdell and Barzillai Ray. Thomas Nickerson's position as Chase's after oarsman meant that he was not included in this
group but must manage as best he could on the leakiest of the three
boats. From a Nantucketer's perspective, however, Chase's boat was
preferable to Joy's.

Although originally from Nantucket, Joy's family had moved to the recently established whaling port of Hudson, New York. Chase reported that Joy had been suffering from an undiagnosed illness, possibly tuberculosis, well before the sinking. Seriously ill and not a full-fledged Nantucketer, Joy was given only off-islanders. If the success of a group in a survival situation is dependent on strong, active leadership, Joy's six crew members were put at an immediate disadvantage. The Nantucketers had done their best to take care of their own.

All twenty men were nominally under the command of Captain Pollard, but each boat-crew remained an autonomous entity that might at any moment become separated from the others. Each boat was given two hundred pounds of hardtack, sixty-five gallons of water, and two Galapagos tortoises. To ensure that discipline would be maintained even under the most arduous circumstances, Pollard gave each mate a pistol and some powder, keeping a musket for himself.

At 12:30—less than a half hour after the officers had convened their council—they set out in a strong breeze, their schooner-rigged whale-boats, according to Nickerson, "a very handsome show on this our first start." The men's spirits were the lowest they'd ever been. With the *Essex* receding rapidly behind them, they were beginning to appreciate what Nickerson called "the slender thread upon which our lives were hung."

All were affected by leaving their ship for the last time. Even the stoic Chase could not help but wonder at how "we looked upon our shattered and sunken vessel with such an excessive fondness and regret . . . [I]t seemed as if abandoning her we had parted with all hope." The men exchanged frightened glances, even as they continued to search out the disappearing wreck, "as though," Nickerson said, "it were possible that she could relieve us from the fate that seemed to await us."

By four o'clock that afternoon, they had lost sight of the *Essex*. Almost immediately, the men's morale began to improve. Nickerson sensed that, no longer haunted by the vision of the disabled ship, "[we had been] relieved from a spell by which we had been bound." He went so far as to claim that "now that our minds were made up for the worst, half the struggle was over." With no turning back, they had only one chance—to hold to their plan.

7

At Sea

As darkness approached at the end of the first day, the wind built steadily, kicking up a steep, irregular chop. The *Essex* whaleboats were hybrids—built for rowing but now adapted to sail—and the men were still learning how they handled. Instead of a rudder, each boat was equipped with a steering oar. This eighteen-foot lever enabled a rowed whaleboat to spin around in its own length, but it was not so effective in guiding a sailboat, and required the helmsman to stand at the cumbersome oar. At this early stage in the voyage, the whaleboats were dangerously overloaded. Instead of five hundred pounds of whaling equipment, each boat contained close to a thousand pounds of bread, water, and tortoises, and waves broke over the built-up gunwales and soaked the men.

Each boat-crew was divided into two watches. While half the men attempted to rest—curling up with the Galapagos tortoises in the bilge or leaning uncomfortably against the seats—the others steered, tended the sails, and bailed. They also attempted to keep an eye on the other boats, which would sometimes disappear entirely from view when they dipped down into the trough, or bottom, of a wave.

At the start it had been decided that every effort would be made to keep the three boats together. Together they could help if one of them ran into trouble; together they could keep one another's spirits up. "[U]naided, and unencouraged by each other," Chase observed, "there were with us many whose weak minds, I am confident, would have sunk under the dismal retrospections of the past catastrophe, and who did not possess either sense or firmness enough to contemplate our approaching destiny, without the cheering of some more determined countenance than their own."

There was also a more practical reason for staying together: there was not enough navigational equipment to go around. Pollard and Chase each had a compass, a quadrant, and a copy of Bowditch's *Navigator*, but Joy had nothing. If his boat-crew should become separated from the other two, they would be unable to find their way across the ocean.

Night came on. Although moon and starlight still made it possible to detect the ghostly paleness of the whaleboats' sails, the men's field of vision shrank dramatically in the darkness.

Even at night the crews were able to maintain a lively three-way conversation among the boats. The subject on everyone's mind was of course the "means and prospects of our deliverance." It was agreed that their best chance of survival lay in meeting a whaleship. The *Essex* had sunk about three hundred miles north of the Offshore Ground. They still had about five days of sailing before they entered the Ground, where, they desperately hoped, they would come across a whaler.

That first night of their journey, Chase, Pollard, and Joy distributed the rations of bread and water to their boat-crews. It was two days after the sinking now, and the men's interest in food had finally returned; the bread was quickly eaten. Each man would get six ounces of hardtack and half a pint of water a day. Hardtack was a simple dried bread made out of flour and water. Baked into a moisture-free rock to prevent spoilage, hardtack had to be broken into small pieces or soaked in water before it was eaten, if a sailor didn't want to crack a tooth.

The daily ration was equivalent to six slices of bread, and it provided about five hundred calories. Chase estimated that this amounted to less than a third of the nourishment required by "an ordinary man."

Modern dietary analysis indicates that for a five-foot, eight-inch person weighing 145 pounds, these provisions met about a quarter of his daily energy needs. True, the men of the *Essex* had more than just bread; they had tortoises. Each tortoise was a pod of fresh meat, fat, and blood that was capable of providing as many as 4,500 calories per man—the equivalent of nine days of hardtack. Yet, even augmented by the tortoises, their daily rations amounted to a starvation diet. If they did succeed in reaching South America in sixty days, each man knew he would be little more than a breathing skeleton.

But as they would soon discover, their greatest concern was not food but rather water. The human body, which is 70 percent water, requires a bare minimum of a pint a day to remove its waste products. The men of the *Essex* would have to make do with half that daily amount. If they experienced any hot weather, the deficit would only increase.

➤   ➤   ➤

The next morning, the men were greatly relieved to discover that after a night of high winds all three boats were still close together. The wind built throughout the day, requiring them to shorten sail. The boats' sails could be easily adapted to the changing conditions, and after the sails were taken in, Chase reported, the men "did not apprehend any very great danger from the then violence of the wind." The high seas, however, continued to pound them. Constantly wet from the salt spray, they had begun to develop painful sores on their skin that the violent bouncing of the boats only worsened.

In his sea chest, Chase found an assortment of useful items: a jackknife, a whetstone, three small fish hooks, a cake of soap, a suit of clothes, a pencil, and ten sheets of writing paper. As first mate, Chase had been responsible for keeping the *Essex*'s log, and using the pencil and paper he now attempted to start "a sort of sea journal"—despite the horrendous conditions. "It was with much difficulty . . . that

I could keep any sort of record," Chase remembered, "owing to the incessant rocking and unsteadiness of the boat and the continual dashing of spray of the sea over us."

There were other daily rituals. Every morning they shaved with the same knife Chase used to sharpen his pencil. Benjamin Lawrence spent a portion of each day twisting stray strands of rope into an ever-lengthening piece of twine. The boatsteerer vowed that if he should ever get out of the whaleboat alive, he would save the string as a memorial to the ordeal.

At noon they paused to take an observation. Determining the angle of the sun with a quadrant was not easy on a tiny, wave-tossed boat. Their best estimate put them at latitude 0°58' south. It was an encouraging indication. They had not only crossed back over the equator but had traveled approximately seventy-one nautical miles since leaving the wreck the day before, putting them ahead of their daily target of sixty miles. In the afternoon the wind moderated, enabling them to shake out the sails and dry their wet clothes in the sun.

That day Pollard decided to abandon "the idea altogether of keeping any correct longitudinal reckoning." To maintain an accurate estimate of a vessel's position, it is necessary to keep track of both its north-to-south position, or latitude, and its east-to-west position, or longitude. A noon observation with a quadrant indicates only a craft's latitude. If a navigator in 1820 had a chronometer—an exceptionally accurate timepiece adapted to the rigors of being stored on a ship— he could compare the time of his noon sight with the time in Greenwich, England, and calculate his longitude. But chronometers at this time were expensive and not yet widely used on Nantucket whaleships.

The alternative was to perform what was called a lunar observation, or simply a lunar. This was an extremely complicated process that involved as many as three hours of calculations before the vessel's longitude could be determined—an impossibility on a whaleboat. Besides, according to Nickerson, Pollard had not yet learned how to work a lunar.

That left dead reckoning. The officers of every ship kept a careful record of its heading, as indicated by the compass, and its speed. Speed was determined by throwing a knotted length of rope with a piece of wood at the end of it (called a log line) into the water and determining how much of it (that is, how many "knots") ran out in a set period of time. An hourglass, known as a slowglass, was used to measure the time. The ship's speed and direction were recorded, and this information was transferred onto a chart, where the captain established the ship's estimated position.

Chase explained that "having no glass, nor log-line," they decided that it was futile to maintain an estimate of their longitude. If Pollard's inability to work a lunar is any indication, he was not a particularly skilled navigator or an unusually unskilled one. There were many captains who were also navigating their vessels by dead reckoning and, like Pollard, never expected to find themselves in such a situation. By forgoing all estimates of their longitude, he and his men were now sailing blind, with no way to determine their distance from South America.

➤   ➤   ➤

By the morning of Friday, November 24, the third day in the boats, the waves were "very large," according to Chase, "and increased, if possible, the extreme uncomfortableness of our situation." Nickerson observed that if they'd been aboard the *Essex*, the wind would have seemed unexceptional, but now, he said, "in our crippled state it answers the purpose of a gale, and keeps us constantly wet and chilled through." That day an immense wave broke over Chase's boat and almost filled it with water. The swamped boat threatened to roll over on its side as kegs, tortoises, and Chase's sea chest floated up from the bottom and knocked against the men. They bailed frantically, knowing that the next wave might sink them.

Once they'd brought the boat out of danger, they discovered that some of the hardtack—which they'd carefully wrapped in sailcloth—had been soaked by the seawater. They did their best to salvage as much of the damaged bread as possible. Over the course of the next few days, they would seize every chance to dry the dissolving lumps in the sun. While this saved the provisions from what Nickerson called "utter ruin," the bread remained infiltrated with salt, the worst possible thing for their already water-deprived bodies. "The bread being our only dependence," Nickerson remembered, "[this] gave . . . us on the whole a cheerless prospect"—a prospect that only worsened when they learned that a portion of the bread on Pollard's boat had also been damaged. A few days before, the officers had possessed cautious faith in "the human means at our command"; now they recognized "our utter dependence on that divine aid we so much the more stood in need of."

At eight o'clock the next morning, the man assigned to bailing Chase's boat became alarmed. Try as he might, he couldn't keep ahead of the rising tide of water. Their boat, he alerted the rest of the crew, was sinking. Soon all six men were searching for the new leak, their hands probing desperately in the sloshing bilge, feeling the boat's sides for the gush of incoming water. It wasn't until they'd torn up the floor that they discovered the problem: one of the planks in the bow had sprung from the hull, and water was pouring in. The leak was about six inches below the waterline, and if they were going to fix it, they needed to figure out some way to get at it from the outside.

The sprung board was on the starboard side, and Chase immediately "hove about," using the steering oar to turn the boat so that the wind was now coming over the other side. This put the leak on the windward, or "high," side; Chase hoped to heel the boat over enough so that the hole would rise up out of the water.

Noticing that Chase had suddenly veered away, Pollard brought his own boat around and headed for the first mate. After shortening sail, Pollard came alongside and asked what was wrong.

Now that the captain's boat was beside them, Chase ordered his own crew to move to the port side and as far aft as possible, raising the bow up into the air and out of the water. Working from Pollard's boat, the first mate and captain attempted to steady the bow, realign the board, and hammer it into place. There was little room for error. The end of the board was already riddled with old nail holes, and it was critical that they drive in each new nail cleanly. Even though they were being bounced up and down by the waves, Chase and Pollard managed "to drive in a few nails, and secured [the plank], much beyond our expectations." Soon all three boats were once again sailing to the south.

"This little incident, although it may seem small," Nickerson recalled, "[caused] amongst us the greatest excitement." With a clear demonstration that their whaleboats might fall apart around them at any time, the men felt "a great gloominess over the natural prospects of our deliverance." They knew that the longer the ordeal lasted, the more the boats would suffer in "the heavy and repeated racking of the swell." All it took was the loss of a single nail, and one of these boats might be lost forever.

For the men in Chase's crew it had been an especially trying day. That evening Richard Peterson, the sole African American on their boat, led them in prayers and a few hymns. Nickerson remembered how the words and songs of the "pious old colored man . . . drew our minds from our present miseries to seek deliverance from a higher power." That comfort notwithstanding, by the morning of November 26, the tentative optimism with which the men had begun the boat voyage had eroded into despair.

➤   ➤   ➤

That night, at about eleven o'clock, Chase lay down in the bottom of his boat to sleep. He had just nodded off when he was startled awake by a cry from one of his men. Captain Pollard, the man said, was calling out to them in the darkness. Chase sat up and listened. In the howling wind and breaking waves, he could hear Pollard shouting to Joy, whose boat was nearest to him. Chase tacked around and sailed for the other two boats, only dimly visible in the moonless dark, and asked what was wrong. Given what had happened to the *Essex* only a week before, the reply seemed like a sick joke.

Pollard told them that his boat had been attacked by a whale.

Instead of a sperm whale, it had been a smaller, but more aggressive, killer whale. These eight- to twelve-ton toothed whales feed on warm-blooded animals such as dolphins and seals. They hunt in packs and have even been known to attack and kill sperm whales. There have been documented cases in which killer whales, also known as orcas, have repeatedly rammed and sunk wooden sailing yachts.

Pollard explained that, entirely unprovoked, the whale had slammed its head against their boat and taken a sizable bite out of it. Then it proceeded to "play about" the boat, batting it around with its head and tail as a cat might toy with a mouse, before it finally attacked once again, this time splitting the boat's stem. As the whale churned up the water around them, the men grabbed the two poles that held up the tips of the sails (known as sprit poles) and repeatedly punched the creature's sides. Chase arrived just as Pollard and his men succeeded in beating back the whale and sending it swimming away.

Pollard's boat had begun to swamp, so he ordered his crew to transfer their provisions to the other boats. All night the three boats lay huddled together. Unable to see very far in the inky darkness, the men let their imaginations fill the void with their fears. Over the last week they had contended with stiff headwinds, spoiled provisions, and leaky boats. To be attacked by yet another whale was the ultimate blow: "[I]t seemed to us as if fate was wholly relentless, in pursuing us with such a cruel complication of disasters." They searched the water's black surface, convinced that the whale would reappear. "We were not without our fears that the fish might renew his attack, some time during the night, upon one of the other boats, and unexpectedly destroy us." Without their ship to protect them, the hunters had become the prey.

➤ ➤ ➤

The next morning they accomplished a quick repair of Pollard's boat by nailing thin strips of wood along the interior of the broken section. Once again, they were on their way, this time in a strong southeasterly breeze. That day the men in Chase's boat began to experience overpowering sensations of thirst—a lust for water that made it impossible to think about anything else. Despite the dryness of their mouths, they talked compulsively about their cravings. Only gradually did they realize the cause of their distress.

The day before, they had started eating the saltwater-damaged bread. The bread, which they had carefully dried in the sun, now contained all the salt of seawater but not, of course, the water. Already severely dehydrated, the men were, in effect, pouring gasoline on the fire of their thirsts—forcing their kidneys to extract additional fluid from their bodies to excrete the salt. They were beginning to suffer from a condition known as hypernatremia, in which an excessive amount of sodium can bring on convulsions.

"The privation of water is justly ranked among the most dreadful of the miseries of our life," Chase recorded. "[T]he violence of raving thirst has no parallel in the catalogue of human calamities." Chase claimed that it was on this day, November 28—the sixth since leaving the wreck—that "our extreme sufferings here first commenced."

Even after they realized that the bread was responsible for their agony, the men in the first mate's boat resolved to continue eating the damaged provisions. The bread would spoil if it wasn't eaten soon, and their plan was contingent on a full sixty days of provisions. "Our determination was, to suffer as long as human patience and endurance would hold out," Chase wrote, "having only in view, the relief that would be afforded us, when the quantity of wet provisions should be exhausted."

The next day it became clear that the strain of sailing in the open ocean, day and night, for more than a week had taken its toll on the boats. The seams were gradually pulling apart, and all three craft now had to be bailed constantly. On board Chase's boat the situation was the most dire, but the first mate refused to give in. With his hammer in hand, he attended to even the most trivial repair. "[B]eing an active and ingenious man," Nickerson recalled, the first mate let "no opportunity pass whereby he [could] add a nail by way of strengthening" the boat's ribs and planks. The constant activity helped to divert Chase's men from the reality of their situation. They were in the worst of the three boats, but they had a leader who had dedicated himself to postponing its disintegration until it was beyond his final powers to prevent it.

By the following day, the men's hunger had become almost as difficult to bear as their thirst. The weather proved the best they'd seen since leaving the *Essex* eight days before, and Chase proposed that they attempt to allay "the ravenous gnawings upon our stomachs" by eating one of the tortoises. All the men readily agreed, and at one o'clock that afternoon, Chase's dissection began. First they flipped the tortoise on its back. As his men held its beak and claws, Chase slit the creature's throat, cutting the arteries and veins on either side of the vertebrae in the neck. Nickerson claimed that "all seemed quite impatient of the opportunity to drink the blood as it came oozing from the wound of the sacrificed animal."

They collected the blood in the same tin cup from which they drank their water rations. Despite their shrieking thirst, some of the men could not make themselves drink the blood. For his part, Chase "took it like a medicine to relieve the extreme dryness of my palate."

All of them, however, were willing to eat. Chase inserted his knife into the leathery skin beside the neck and worked his way around the shell's edge, cutting with a sawing motion until he could lift out the meat and guts. With the help of the tinderbox stored in the whaleboat's small keg of emergency equipment, they kindled a fire in the shell and cooked the tortoise, "entrails and all."

After ten days of eating only bread, the men greedily attacked the tortoise, their teeth ripping the succulent flesh as warm juice ran down their salt-encrusted faces. Their bodies' instinctive need for nutrition led them irresistibly to the tortoise's vitamin-rich heart and liver. Chase dubbed it "an unspeakably fine repast."

Their hunger was so voracious that once they began to eat, they found it difficult to stop. An average-sized tortoise would have provided each man with about three pounds of meat, one pound of fat, and at least half a cup of blood, together worth more than 4,500 calories—equivalent to a large Thanksgiving dinner. This would have been a tremendous amount of food to introduce into the shrunken stomach of a person who had only eaten a total of four pounds of bread over the last ten days. The men's dehydrated condition would have also made it difficult for their stomachs to generate the digestive juices required to handle the large amount of food. But neither Chase nor Nickerson speaks of saving any of the cooked tortoise for a later day. For these starved men, this was one gratification no one was willing to delay. "[O]ur bodies were considerably recruited," Chase wrote, "and I felt my spirits now much higher than they had been at any time before." Instead of limiting each whaleboat to two live tortoises, they now realized, they should have butchered and cooked the meat of every animal they found on the wreck.

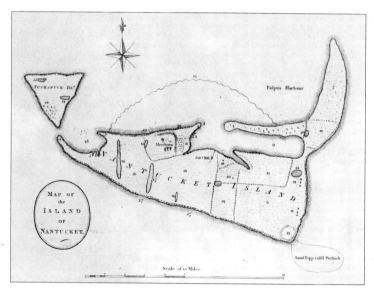

This map of Nantucket, drawn by the town's sheriff, appeared in Hector
St. John de Crèvecoeur's *Letters from an American Farmer* (1782). The somewhat
fanciful shape of Nantucket's main harbor, labeled "9" on the map, suggests
that Nantucketers' preoccupation with the sperm whale influenced their
image of their own island. *(Geography and Map Division, Library of Congress, Washington, D.C.)*

Nantucket in the early nineteenth century. The two-wheeled cart in the
foreground was known as a "calash." *(Courtesy of the Nantucket Historical Association.)*

The *Essex*'s shipping paper, 1817. Of the men listed in this crew, George Pollard, Thomas Chappel, Owen Chase, Obed Hendricks, and Benjamin Lawrence would return for the final voyage in 1819.

(Photo by Terry Pommett. Courtesy of the Nantucket Historical Association.)

A scene of whale hunting in the Pacific Ocean, 1834. The print is by William Huggins. *(New Bedford Whaling Museum.)*

This scene from J. Ross Browne's *Etchings of a Whaling Cruise* (1846) shows hungry sailors fighting for a piece of salt junk.

(General Research Division, The New York Public Library, Astor, Lenox and Tilden Foundations.)

A late twentieth-century rendering of the *Essex* rounding Great Point, Nantucket, August 1819. *(Painting by L. F. Tantillo © 1999.)*

A crew list of the *Essex*'s final voyage, found pasted to a page in an old scrapbook, revealed for the first time the name of the black sailor who deserted in South America (Henry DeWitt, listed as "runaway").

(Photo by Terry Pommett. Courtesy of the Nantucket Historical Association.)

An early twentieth-century photograph of a whaleboat being lowered into the water. An experienced crew could launch a fully rigged whaleboat in under a minute. (*Robert Cushman Murphy Collection. © Mystic Seaport, Mystic, CT.*)

A well-known depiction of a boatsteerer lancing a sperm whale. Once the whalemen had dragged their boat close to the whale, the boatsteerer would kill the whale by stabbing at its vital organs with a killing lance. The rough seas and the whale's tail only add to the difficulty of this maneuver.

(© Mystic Seaport, Mystic, CT.)

Whalemen on a "Nantucket sleigh ride." After a whale was stabbed by a harpoon, the whale typically dragged the whaleboat along at speeds of fifteen to twenty knots, making the whalemen for that moment the fastest sailors in the world.

(Robert Cushman Murphy Collection. © Mystic Seaport, Mystic, CT.)

In December 1997, a sperm whale washed up on Nantucket's Low Beach. Here, Rick Morcam uses a boarding knife from the Nantucket Whaling Museum to cut away a strip of blubber as a chain rips the blubber from the whale's body. *(Photo by Jim Powers. Courtesy of the Nantucket Inquirer and Mirror.)*

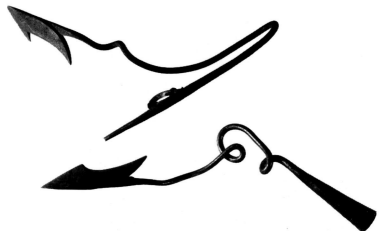

As the whalemen clung to the rope attached to a harpoon lodged in the whale's thick blubber, the pressure was enough to bend solid steel, as shown by this photograph of two mangled harpoons removed from a slaughtered whale (of a different and later design than those used aboard the *Essex*). *(New Bedford Whaling Museum.)*

This eighteen-foot sperm whale jaw at the Nantucket Whaling Museum was taken from a whale thought to have been about eighty feet long—slightly smaller than the whale that attacked the *Essex*. (*Photo by Terry Pommett. Courtesy of the Nantucket Historical Association.*)

This illustration from the Russell-Purrington Panorama—a series of paintings intended to describe the workings of whale hunting—shows the attack of the whale on the *Essex*.   *(New Bedford Whaling Museum.)*

OPPOSITE, ABOVE: Nickerson's sketch of the whale attacking the *Essex*. Chase and other members of the crew are shown already beginning to untie the spare whaleboat from the rack above the quarterdeck.

(Photo by Terry Pommett. Courtesy of the Nantucket Historical Association.)

OPPOSITE, BELOW: After the *Essex* filled up with water and fell over onto her side, the sailors cut the sails and chopped off a portion of each mast, allowing the ship to float upright again at a forty-five degree angle.

(Photo by Terry Pommett. Courtesy of the Nantucket Historical Association.)

This Sketch shows the Ship at the moment of attack, with the whale
2 miles under the Ships lee and arrived a Shoal of whales with whale boats

Ship Essex as She appeared On the morning of Nov 20th at 8 A.M.

This Sketch is designed to show the Ship one hour after
when the Shrouds were Cut and the masts broken & falling with all Sails Set
the Ship at an angle of 45 Degrees & water Logged.

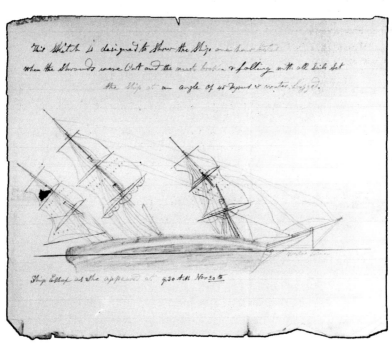

Ship Essex as She appeared at 9.50 A.M. Nov 20th

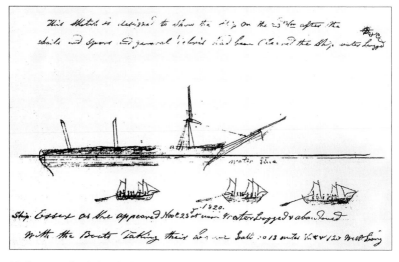

Nickerson's final sketch shows the three whaleboats—now rigged for sailing with their sides built up by half a foot—leaving the wreck.

(Photo by Terry Pommett. Courtesy of the Nantucket Historical Association.)

Sensational accounts and representations of native cannibalism, such as this from Theodor de Bry's *Historia Americae* (1634), contributed to the whalemen's fears concerning the inhabitants of the South Sea islands. *(By permission of the British Library. G.6627, page 179.)*

A photograph of sailors in 1913 lowering sail on a whaleboat. The *Essex* whale-boats were rigged with an extra aft sail and a jib at the bow, making the boats even more cramped (we only see four sailors in this boat, compared with six in the *Essex* boats). *(Robert Cushman Murphy Collection. © Mystic Seaport, Mystic, CT.)*

Henderson Island, looking toward what is known today as North West Beach. The *Essex* men camped on North Beach, directly behind the photographer. From here, three boats set out for South America, three thousand miles to the east.

(© *T. G. Benton, University of Stirling, U.K.*)

Owen Chase, a proud and handsome Nantucket whaling captain at the peak of his career.

(Courtesy of the Tice-Woodward Collection.)

Also reputed to be Owen Chase, some time after the *Essex* disaster. As Chase grew older, the headaches that had plagued him ever since the ordeal became unbearable. By 1868 he was judged insane.

(Courtesy of the Nantucket Historical Association.)

Thomas Nickerson, many years after his *Essex* voyage. After moving to Brooklyn, New York, where he pursued a career in the merchant service, Nickerson returned to Nantucket in the 1870s, living out his retirement as the proprietor of a boardinghouse.

(Courtesy of the Nantucket Historical Association.)

This small chest, reputed to be from the whaleship *Essex*, was found floating in the vicinity of the wreck. It was purchased by John Taber of Providence, Rhode Island. In 1896, Taber's daughter donated the chest to the Nantucket Historical Association.

(Photo by Terry Pommett. Courtesy of the Nantucket Historical Association.)

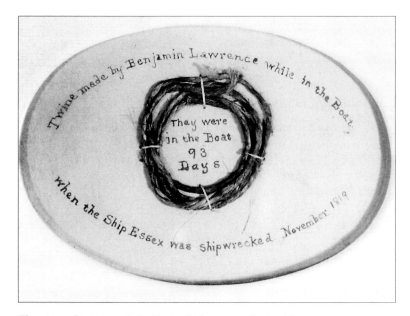

The piece of twine made by Benjamin Lawrence during his three months in an *Essex* whaleboat.

(Photo by Terry Pommett. Courtesy of the Nantucket Historical Association.)

For the first time in several days, the sky was clear enough for a noon observation. Pollard's sight indicated that they were approaching latitude 8° south. Since leaving the wreck on November 22, they had traveled almost five hundred miles, putting them slightly ahead of schedule—at least in terms of distance sailed over the water. That evening, with the bones of the tortoise littering the boat's bilge, Richard Peterson once again led the men in prayer.

>   >   >

For the next three days, the weather remained mild and clear. The wind shifted to the north, allowing them to shape their course toward Peru. Their stomachs full, they dared to believe that "our situation was not at that moment . . . so comfortless as we had been led at first to consider." Nickerson noticed "a degree of repose and carelessness, scarcely to be looked for amid persons in our forlorn and hopeless situation."

Only one thing lay between them and "a momentary forgetfulness of our actual situation"—a ferocious, unbearable thirst. Chase reported that even after consuming the tortoise and its blood, they still yearned for a long, cool drink of water: "[H]ad it not been for the pains which that gave us, we should have tasted, during this spell of fine weather, a species of enjoyment."

On Sunday, December 3, they ate the last of their damaged bread. For the men in Chase's boat, it was a turning point. At first they didn't notice the change, but with each succeeding day of eating unspoiled hardtack, "the moisture began to collect in our mouths and the parching fever of the palate imperceptibly left it." They were still seriously dehydrated, and becoming only more so, but no longer were they introducing excessive amounts of salt into their bodies.

That evening, after the men in Chase's boat had conducted what Nickerson called "our usual prayer meeting," clouds moved in, cutting them off from the starlight. At around ten o'clock, Chase and

Pollard lost track of Joy's boat. Its disappearance was so sudden that Nickerson feared "something had destroyed them." Almost immediately, Chase turned around and raised a lantern to the masthead as the rest of his crew scanned the darkness for some sign of the second mate's boat. About a quarter of a mile to leeward, they spotted a small light flickering in the gloom. It proved to be Joy's answering signal. All three boats were once again accounted for.

Two nights later, it was Chase's turn to become separated from the others. Instead of lighting a lantern, the first mate fired his pistol. Soon after, Pollard and Joy appeared out of the darkness to windward. That night the officers agreed that if they should ever become separated again, no action would be taken to reassemble the convoy. Too much time was being lost trying to keep the boats together. Besides, if one of the boats either capsized or became unrepairable, there was little the other crews could do. All three boats were already overloaded, and to add any more men would result in the eventual deaths of all of them. The prospect of beating away the helpless crew of another boat with their oars was awful to contemplate, even if they all realized that each boat should go it alone.

However, so strong was what Chase called "the extraordinary interest which we felt in each other's company" that none of them would consider voluntarily separating. This "desperate instinct" persisted to such a point that, even in the midst of conditions that made simply staying afloat a full-time occupation, they "continued to cling to each other with a strong and involuntary impulse."

They still had thousands of miles left to go if they were to reach their destination. They were starving and thirsty. Their boats were barely holding together. But there was a way out.

On December 9, well into their third week in the open boats, they drew abreast of the Society Islands. If they had headed west, sailing along latitude 17° south, they would have reached Tahiti, perhaps in as little as a week. There were islands in the Tuamotu Archipelago that they might have sighted in less than half that time. They would have also been sailing *with* the wind and waves, easing the strain on the boats.

However, despite the numerous setbacks they had already faced, despite the extremity of their sufferings, Pollard, Chase, and Joy pushed on with the original plan. Nickerson could not understand why. "I can only say there was gross ignorance or a great oversight somewhere, which cost many . . . fine seamen their lives." The men's sufferings only narrowed and intensified their focus. It was "up the coast" or nothing.

8

THIRST

On the eighteenth day since leaving the wreck, the men's thirst and hunger reached a new, agonizing level. Even the stoic Chase was tempted "to violate our resolution, and satisfy, for once, the hard yearnings of nature from our stock." Raiding their stores, however, would be a death sentence: "[A] little reflection served to convince us of the imprudence and unmanliness of the measure, and it was abandoned with a sort of melancholy effort of satisfaction."

Just to make sure that no one was tempted to steal any of the bread, Chase transferred the provisions to his sea chest. Whenever he slept, he made sure to have an arm or a leg draped across it. He also kept the loaded pistol at his side. For a man from the Quaker island of Nantucket, it was an unusual display of force. Nickerson's impression was that "nothing but violence to his person" would have led the first mate to surrender the provisions. Chase decided that if anyone should object to his method of rationing, he would immediately divide up the hardtack into equal portions and distribute it among the men. If it came down to giving up his own stock, he was "resolved to make the consequences of it fatal."

That afternoon, a school of flying fish surrounded the three whaleboats. Four of the fish hit the sails of Chase's boat. One fell at the first mate's feet and, instinctively, he devoured it whole, scales and all. As the rest of the crew scrambled for the other three fish, Chase found himself inclined to laugh for the first time since the sinking of the *Essex* at "the ludicrous and almost desperate efforts of my five companions,

who each sought to get a fish." The first mate might insist on the disciplined sharing of the bread and water, but a different standard pre-
vailed when it came to gifts like flying fish—then, it was every man
for himself.

The next day the wind dropped to almost nothing, and Chase proposed that they eat their second tortoise. As had happened eleven days
earlier, the "luxuriant repast . . . invigorated our bodies, and gave a
fresh flow to our spirits." Over the next three days, the wind remained
light. The temperature climbed and the men languished beneath a
cloudless sky. "[H]aving no way of screening ourselves from [the
sun's] piercing rays," Nickerson wrote, "our suffering became most
intolerable as our short allowance of water was barely enough to
support life."

By December 14, the twenty-third day since leaving the *Essex*, they
were rapidly approaching their deadline for reaching the variables. But
they were stuck in a calm, with hundreds of miles still to go to the
south. If they were to have any hope of reaching the coast alive, their
provisions would have to last them considerably longer than sixty
days. Chase announced to his men that he was cutting their rations of
hardtack in half, to only three ounces a day. He studied his crew carefully, looking for any signs of resistance. "No objections were made to
this arrangement," Chase reported. "[A]ll submitted, or seemed to do
so, with an admirable fortitude and forbearance."

Even though their supply of water was in even greater danger of
running out, Chase had no alternative but to maintain their daily ration at half a pint. "[Our] thirst had become now incessantly more intolerable than our hunger," he wrote, "and the quantity then allowed
was barely sufficient to keep the mouth in a state of moisture, for
about one third of the time."

In 1906, W. J. McGee, director of the St. Louis Public Museum, published one of the most detailed and graphic descriptions of the ravages

of extreme dehydration ever recorded. McGee's account was based on the experiences of Pablo Valencia, a forty-year-old sailor-turned-prospector, who survived almost seven days in the Arizona desert without water. The only liquid Valencia drank during his ordeal was the few drops of moisture he was able to extract from a scorpion and his own urine, which he collected each day in his canteen.

The men of the *Essex* were driven to similar extremes. "In vain was every expedient tried to relieve the raging fever of the throat," Chase recalled. They knew that drinking saltwater would only worsen their condition, but this did not stop some of them from attempting to hold small quantities of it in their mouths, hoping that they might absorb some of the moisture. It only increased their thirst. Like Valencia, they drank their urine. "Our suffering during these calm days," Chase wrote, "almost exceeded human belief."

The *Essex* survivors had entered what McGee describes as the "cotton-mouth" phase of thirst. Saliva becomes thick and foul-tasting; the tongue clings irritatingly to the teeth and the roof of the mouth. Even though speech is difficult sufferers are often moved to complain ceaselessly about their thirst until their voices become so cracked and hoarse that they can speak no more. A lump seems to form in the throat, causing the sufferer to swallow repeatedly in a vain attempt to dislodge it. Severe pain is felt in the head and neck. The face feels full due to the shrinking of the skin. Hearing is affected, and many people begin to hallucinate.

Still to come for the *Essex* crew were the agonies of a mouth that has ceased to generate saliva. The tongue hardens into what McGee describes as "a senseless weight, swinging on the still-soft root and striking foreignly against the teeth." Speech becomes impossible, although sufferers are known to moan and bellow. Next is the "blood sweats" phase, involving "a progressive mummification of the initially living body." The tongue swells to such proportions that it squeezes past the jaws. The eyelids crack and the eyeballs begin to weep tears of blood. The throat is so swollen that breathing becomes difficult, creating a terrifying sensation of drowning. Finally, as the power of the sun draws the remaining moisture from the body, there is "living death," the state into which Pablo Valencia had entered when McGee discovered him on a desert trail, crawling on his hands and knees.

Thanks to their daily half pint of water, the men of the *Essex* had not yet reached this point—but they were deteriorating rapidly. As the sun beat down out of an empty blue sky, the heat became so intolerable that three of the men in Chase's boat decided to hang over the gunwale and cool their blistered bodies in the sea. Almost as soon as the first man dropped over the side, he shouted with excitement. The bottom of their boat was covered with what he described as small clams. He quickly pulled one off and ate it, pronouncing it a "most delicious and agreeable food."

Actually not clams, these were gooseneck barnacles. Unlike the whitish, cone-shaped barnacles commonly seen on docks and ships, goosenecks have a dark brown shell surrounding a fleshy, pinkish-white neck. A medieval myth claimed that once these barnacles grew to a sufficient size, they would transform themselves into geese and fly away. Today the Coast Guard uses the size of the gooseneck barnacles growing on the bottom of a derelict craft to determine how long the vessel has been at sea. They can grow to half a foot in length, but the barnacles on Chase's whaleboat were probably not much more than a few inches long.

Soon all six men were plucking the crustaceans off the boat's bottom and popping them into their mouths "like a set of gluttons." Gooseneck barnacles have long been considered a delicacy in Morocco, Portugal, and Spain, and are farmed commercially today in the state of Washington. Connoisseurs, who eat the tubelike neck only after peeling off the outer skin, compare the taste to crab, lobster, or shrimp. The *Essex* men, not as picky, consumed everything but the shells.

"[A]fter having satisfied the immediate craving of the stomach," Chase wrote, "we gathered large quantities and laid them up in the boat." But getting the men back aboard proved a problem. They were too weak to pull themselves over the gunwale. Luckily, the three men who couldn't swim had elected to remain on the boat and were able to haul the others in. They had intended to save the uneaten goose-necks for another day. But after less than a half hour of staring at the delectable morsels, they surrendered to temptation and ate them all.

Except for flying fish, gooseneck barnacles would be the only marine life the *Essex* crew would manage to harvest from the open ocean. Indeed, these twenty whalemen were singularly unsuccessful in catching the fish that castaways normally depend on for survival. Part of the problem was that their search for the band of variable winds had taken them into a notoriously sterile region of the Pacific, almost devoid of fish and birds. The three *Essex* whaleboats were now in the heart of the Desolate Region. Like Pablo Valencia, they had journeyed into their very own valley of death.

➤   ➤   ➤

The calm continued into December 15, the twenty-fourth day of the ordeal. Despite the windless conditions, Chase's boat was taking on even more water than usual. Their search for the leak once again prompted them to pull up the floorboards in the bow. This time they discovered that a plank next to the keel, at the very bottom of the boat, had pulled loose. If they had been on the deck of the *Essex*, they would have simply flipped the boat over and renailed the plank. But now, in the middle of the ocean, they had no way of reaching the underside of the boat. Even Chase, whom Nickerson described as their boat's "doctor," could not figure out a way to repair it.

After a few moments' consideration, the twenty-one-year-old boatsteerer Benjamin Lawrence ventured a proposal. He would tie a rope around his waist and dive underwater with the boat's hatchet in his hand. As Chase hammered in a nail from the inside of the boat, Lawrence would hold the hatchet against the outside of the plank. When the tip of the nail hit the metal face of the hatchet, it would curl up like a fishhook and be driven back into the boat. The last blows of Chase's hammer would set the head of the nail while drawing the planks tightly together. This was known as clenching a nail and was usually performed with a tool known as a backing iron. For now, the hatchet would have to do.

On the *Essex*, Lawrence's abilities as a boatsteerer had been called into question, and he had been forced to surrender the harpoon to his demanding first mate. This time, however, it was Lawrence to whom Chase and the rest of the boat-crew looked for guidance. Chase readily agreed to the plan, and soon Lawrence was in the water, pressing the hatchet up against the bottom of the boat. Just as he had predicted, the sprung plank was drawn in snug. Even Chase had to admit that it "answered the purpose much beyond our expectations."

The oppressive conditions continued through the next day and "bore upon our health and spirits with an amazing force and severity." Some of the men experienced thirst-induced delusions. "The most disagreeable excitements were produced by it," Chase commented, "which added to the disconsolate endurance of the calm, called loudly for some mitigating expedient—some sort of relief to our prolonged sufferings." The need for action intensified when the noon observation revealed that they had drifted ten miles backward in the last twenty-four hours.

All around them, the calm ocean reached out to the curved horizon like the bottom of a shiny blue bowl. Their parched mouths made talking, let alone singing hymns, difficult. The prayer meetings, along with their progress, ceased. That Sunday they sat silently in their boats, desperate for deliverance.

Up until this point, it had been the African Americans, specifically the sixty-year-old Richard Peterson, who had led the men in prayer. This was not uncommon at sea. White sailors often looked to blacks and their evangelical style of worship as sources of religious strength, especially in times of peril.

That afternoon, Pollard was finally moved to speak beneath the punishing sun. His voice ravaged by dehydration, he proposed in a halting rasp that they attempt to row their way out of the calm. Each man would be given double rations during the day, and then that night they would row "until we should get a breeze from some quarter or other."

All readily agreed to the proposal. At last, after days of being stuck as if pinned to a place in the ocean, with nothing to distract them from their thirst and hunger, they had something to prepare for. They ate the bread and felt every sublimely refreshing drop of water seep into their cracked and shriveled mouths. They looked forward to the night ahead.

Under normal circumstances, rowing was a task that helped define each man's worth on a whaleship. Each crew took pride in its ability to row effortlessly, for hours at a time, and nothing made the men happier than passing another boat. But that night any flickering of those competitive fires was soon extinguished. Though in their teens and twenties, they rowed like old men—wincing and groaning with every stroke. For the last three weeks, their bodies had been consuming themselves. Without any natural padding to cushion their bones, they found the simple act of sitting to be a torture. Their arms had shrunk to sticks as their muscles withered, making it difficult to hold, let alone pull, the oars. As man after man collapsed in a slumped heap, it became impossible to continue.

"[W]e made but a very sorry progress," Chase remembered. "Hunger and thirst, and long inactivity, had so weakened us, that in three hours every man gave out, and we abandoned the further prosecution of the plan." Air rattled in their throats and lungs as they lay panting in the boats. Despite the raging heat of their bodies, their thin papery skin was without a hint of perspiration. Gradually the noise of their breathing ebbed, and they were once again deafened by the forbidding silence of a windless and empty ocean.

The next morning they detected a change—a rustling of the water and a movement across their faces as, for the first time in five days, a light breeze poured out across the sea. Even though it was from precisely the wrong direction (southeast), the men welcomed it "with almost frenzied feelings of gratitude and joy."

By noon it was blowing a gale. The wind had veered into the east-southeast, and once again, they were forced to take in all sail and lower the masts. The next day the wind moderated, and soon their sails were pulling them along. Despite the improvement in the weather, that night proved to be, Chase recalled, "one of the most distressing nights in the whole catalogue of our sufferings."

They now knew that even if the wind did miraculously shift into the west, they no longer had enough water to last the thirty or more days it would take to sail to the coast of Chile. Their physical torments had reached a terrible peak. It was almost as if they were being poisoned by the combined effects of thirst and hunger. A thick and bitter saliva collected in their mouths that was "intolerable beyond expression." Their hair was falling out in clumps. Their skin was so burned and covered with sores that a splash of seawater felt like acid burning on their flesh. Strangest of all, as their eyes sunk into their skulls and their cheekbones projected, they all began to look alike, their identities obliterated by dehydration and starvation.

Throughout this long and dismal week, the men had attempted

to sustain themselves with a kind of mantra: " 'Patience and long-suffering' was the constant language of our lips," Chase remembered, "and a determination, strong as the resolves of the soul could make it, to cling to existence as long as hope and breath remained to us." But by the night of December 19, almost precisely a month since the sinking of the *Essex*, several of the men had given up. Chase could see it in their "lagging spirits and worn out frames"—"an utter indifference to their fate." One more day, maybe two, and people would start to die.

The next morning began like so many others. Nickerson recalled how at around seven o'clock, they were "sitting in the bottom of our little boat quite silent and dejected." Nineteen-year-old William Wright, from Cape Cod, stood up to stretch his legs. He glanced out at the sea, then looked again.

"There is land!" he cried.

They see land!

9

THE ISLAND

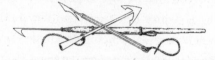

The men in Chase's boat stared eagerly ahead. Ravaged by hunger and thirst, half blinded by glare from the sea and sky, they had seen mirages before, and they feared this might prove to be another. But all of them could see the white sandy beach in the distance. "It was no visionary delusion," Nickerson wrote, "but in reality 'Land Ho.' "

Even the most decrepit of Chase's men sprang to life. "We were all aroused in an instant," the first mate remembered, "as if electrified.... A new and extraordinary impulse now took possession of us. We shook off the lethargy of our senses, and seemed to take another, and a fresh existence." At first glance, the island bore an eerie resemblance to their native Nantucket: a low rise of sand topped with green. Chase called it "a basking paradise before our longing eyes." Nickerson immediately assumed that it marked "the final end to [our] long confinement and sufferings," and added, "Never have my eyes rested on anything so pleasingly beautiful."

It wasn't long before the men in the other two boats had seen the island. Spontaneous cheers rose from their cracked and swollen lips. "It is not within the scope of human calculation," Chase wrote, "to divine what the feelings of our hearts were on this occasion. Alternate expectation, fear, gratitude, surprise, and exultation, each swayed our minds, and quickened our exertions."

By eleven o'clock they were within a quarter mile of the island. They could now see that instead of sand, it was made mostly of rock, with ninety-foot vertical cliffs lining the shore. Beyond the cliffs, the interior of the island was amazingly flat, yet "fresh and green with vegetation." This boded well, they assured themselves, for the presence of ample supplies of water.

Pollard and Chase studied their copies of Bowditch's *Navigator.* Judging from the day's previous observation, they determined it must be Ducie Island at latitude 24°20' south, longitude 124°40' west. After a month at sea, after traveling approximately 1,500 nautical miles, they were farther from the coast of South America than when they had started.

The men's immediate concern was that the island might be inhabited. "In our present state," Nickerson wrote, "we could have made but feeble resistance to an attack from natives." Keeping about a hundred yards from shore, they began sailing around the island. "We . . . frequently fir[ed] a pistol," Nickerson remembered, "as we glided past some valley or nook in the woods to arouse its inhabitants should there be any within hearing. But neither friend nor foe appeared."

The island was an irregular oblong, about six miles long and three miles wide, rimmed by a jagged ledge of rocks and coral. The three boat-crews gradually made their way to the north end. At a bend in the shoreline they found the island's largest beach. "[T]his seemed the most promising position we had seen," Nickerson wrote, "to make an attempt to land with our boats." But first Chase would lead a preliminary scouting party while the three boats stood offshore, just in case they "should unexpectedly find savages in ambush."

Chase, with musket in hand, and two others were dropped off on a large rock. By the time they'd waded ashore, they were already exhausted. "Upon arriving at the beach," the first mate recalled, "it was necessary to take a little breath, and we laid down for a few minutes to rest our weak bodies." They sat on the coarse coral sand, drinking in the sights and sounds of a stunningly beautiful island world. The cliffs behind them were festooned with flowers, shrubs, grasses, and vines. Birds flew about them, seemingly unconcerned by the men's presence. After a month of suffering, they were about to enjoy, Chase was convinced, "a rich banquet of food and drink." But first they had to find a source of water.

They split up, each one hobbling down the uneven beach in a different direction. In an inlet Chase was able to spear an eighteen-inch fish with the ramrod of his musket. He dragged the fish onto the shore and immediately sat down to eat. His two companions joined him, and in less than ten minutes the fish was consumed—"bones, and skin, and scales, and all."

They now imagined they were strong enough to attempt a climb of the cliffs, which they figured to be the most probable source of water. But instead of rocks glistening with moisture, Chase found a dry, scrubby wall of dead coral. The shrubs and vines were not strong enough to support his weight, forcing him to grab the cutting edges of coral. Slashed and bruised, Chase realized he did not have the strength to reach the top.

The euphoria of only a few hours before gave way to the realization that this sterile island of coral might be without drinkable water. If this was true, every second they remained on the island reduced their already slim chances of survival. No matter how tempting it might be to spend at least one night on solid ground, Chase's first inclination was to set sail for South America immediately: "I never for one moment lost sight of the main chance, which I conceived we still had, of either getting to the coast, or of meeting some vessel at sea."

When he returned to the beach he discovered that one of the men had some promising news. He had found a cleft in a rock from which trickled a few droplets of water—just enough to wet his lips, but no more. Perhaps it was advisable to spend the night on the island and devote the next day to searching for water. Chase and his companions went out to the boats, and Chase told Pollard what he thought. They agreed to land.

They dragged the boats up onto a grassy area beneath a stand of trees. "We then turned [the boats] bottom upwards," Nickerson remembered, "thus forming a protection from the night dews." The men fanned out along the shore, and after collecting a few crabs and fish, they settled down beneath the boats, ate their catch, then stretched out their bony limbs for the first time in a month. Sleep soon followed. "[F]ree from all the anxieties of watching and labor," Chase wrote, "[we] gave ourselves up to an unreserved forgetfulness and peace of mind."

Morning came quickly and, with it, a return to the agonies of hunger and thirst. They were now so severely dehydrated that they had begun to lose the ability to speak. "Relief," Chase wrote, "must come soon, or nature would sink." They wandered the beach like ragged skeletons, pausing to lean against trees and rocks to catch their breath. They tried chewing the waxy green leaves of the shrubs that grew in the cliffs, but they were bitter to the taste. They found birds that made no attempt to escape when they plucked them from their nests. In the crevices of the rocks sprouted a grass that, when chewed, produced a temporary flow of moisture in their mouths. But nowhere did they find freshwater.

As soon as they strayed beyond the beach, they discovered that the island was a scrap heap of fractured coral as sharp and piercing as shattered glass. Many of the men had no shoes, which made it impossible for them to explore any great distance from their encampment. They also feared that if they did venture out, they might not have the stamina to return before nightfall, thus exposing themselves "to attacks of wild beasts, which might inhabit the island." That evening they returned, Nickerson wrote, "sorrowing and dejected to our little town of boats in the valley."

But Pollard had a surprise for them. The captain and his steward, William Bond, had spent the day gathering crabs and birds, and by the time the men returned from their searches, Pollard and Bond were in the midst of roasting what Nickerson called "a magnificent repast." Prior to the sinking, food had been a source of dissension between Pollard and his men. Now it was what brought them together, and this time it was the master who was serving his crew. "Here everyone seated himself upon the beautiful green grass," Nickerson remembered, "and perhaps no banquet was ever enjoyed with greater gusto or gave such universal satisfaction."

Pollard had done everything he could that day to increase the health and morale of his men. Chase remained focused on the "main chance": getting to South America and safety. Restless and impatient as always, he had become convinced that they were wasting their time on this island without water. "In this state of affairs, we could not reconcile it to ourselves to remain longer at this place," he wrote. "[A] day, an hour, lost to us unnecessarily here, might cost us our preservation." That evening Chase expressed his concerns to Pollard: "I addressed the substance of these few reflections to the captain, who agreed with me in opinion, upon the necessity of taking some decisive steps in our present dilemma."

While he agreed with his first mate in principle, the captain pointed out that without a new supply of water, their chances of survival were next to nil. To push blindly ahead without exhausting every possibility of finding a spring would be a tragic mistake. "After some considerable conversation on this subject," Chase wrote, "it was finally concluded to spend the succeeding day in the further search for water, and if none should be found, to quit the island the morning after."

➤   ➤   ➤

The men of the *Essex* did not know that they were within just a few hundred miles of saving themselves. Pollard and Chase were mistaken as to their whereabouts. This was not Ducie Island but rather Henderson Island, at virtually the same latitude but seventy miles to the west. Both islands are part of a group named for its most famous member, Pitcairn, an island whose history was inextricably linked with Nantucket. In 1808, a sealing captain from Nantucket named Mayhew Folger stumbled across Pitcairn (whose location was incorrectly recorded on all available navigational guides) and discovered the answer to a nineteen-year-old mystery concerning the notorious mutiny on the *Bounty*.

In 1789, during a voyage to the Pacific, Lieutenant Fletcher Christian led a mutiny against Captain Bligh, commander of the HMS *Bounty*. After abandoning Bligh and those who remained loyal to him in the ship's launch (who would sail 4,000 miles to the island of Timor), the *Bounty* mutineers wandered the Pacific. They picked up some native women and a few men in Tahiti, and eventually made their way to an uninhabited island in the southeastern extreme of Polynesia. In 1820, a small community of *Bounty* descendants was flourishing on Pitcairn. Just four hundred miles to the southwest, a few days' sail from Henderson, they would have provided the *Essex* crew with all the food and water they needed. But Pitcairn was not listed in their Bowditch's *Navigator*. Even if it had been, it's questionable whether they could have found it. As it was, they were off by almost a hundred miles when they tried to determine their current location.

Henderson Island began as a ring of coral enclosing a lagoon, known as an atoll, about 370,000 years ago. Twenty thousand years later, volcanic activity associated with Pitcairn caused the land underneath the atoll to rise. Today, the cliffs of Henderson are between ninety and one hundred feet high and enclose a dry fossil lagoon. Surrounded by a vast ocean, this uninhabited speck of coral might seem an unlikely source of anyone's salvation.

As much as sixty-five inches of rain falls on Henderson each year. This water does not all run off into the sea or evaporate into the air. Much of it seeps down through the thin soils and layers of fossilized coral to create a layer of groundwater. But, unless they could find a spring, all this groundwater would be of no use to the men of the *Essex*.

They weren't the first to be enticed by Henderson and then cheated. Although they weren't aware of it, in the cliffs behind them was a cave in which lay eight human skeletons.

A medical examination performed on the bones in 1966 revealed that they were of Caucasian origin, which suggests that these unidentified people, like the *Essex* crew, had been shipwreck survivors. The examination also revealed that one of the skeletons had belonged to a child between three and five years old. All eight people had died of dehydration.

>   >   >

The next morning—December 22, the thirty-first since leaving the wreck—the men resumed their search for water. Some, like Nickerson, climbed into the cliffs; others investigated the rocks along the beach. Chase returned to where they had found evidence of freshwater two days before. The rock was about a quarter mile from their encampment and, with a hatchet and an old rusted chisel, he and two others made their way across the sand.

"The rock proved to be very soft," Chase wrote, "and in a very short time I had obtained a considerable hole, but, alas! without the least wished-for effect." As the sun rose in the sky, Chase continued to peck away at the rock, hoping that by deepening the hole, he might establish a flow of water. "[B]ut all my hopes and efforts were unavailing," he remembered, "and at last I desisted from further labor, and sat down near it in utter despair."

Then he noticed something curious. On the beach, in the direction of the boats, two men were lugging a container of some sort. He was amazed to see them begin to run. "[T]he idea suddenly darted across my mind," Chase wrote, "that they had found water, and were taking a keg to fill it." Up in the cliffs, Nickerson had noticed the same display of "extraordinary spirit and activity" and soon became part of a general rush for the beach.

The men had, in fact, found a spring bubbling up from a hole in a large flat rock. "The sensation that I experienced was indeed strange, and such as I shall never forget," Chase remembered. "At one instant I felt an almost choking excess of joy, and at the next I wanted the relief of a flood of tears."

By the time Chase reached the spring, men had already begun to drink, eagerly filling their mouths with the miraculous nectar. Mindful that in their dehydrated condition it was dangerous to drink too much water too quickly, Chase urged them to sip only small quantities and to wait several minutes between drinks. But their thirst proved overpowering, and some of the men had to be held back. Despite the officers' best efforts, several of the crew "thoughtlessly swallowed large quantities of [water], until they could drink no more." But the agonizing cramps Chase had warned against never came: "[I]t only served to make them a little stupid and indolent for the remainder of the day."

Once everyone had been given a chance to drink, they began to marvel at their good fortune. The spring was so far below the tide line that it was exposed for just a half hour at dead low tide; at high tide it was as much as six feet underwater. They had time to fill only two small kegs before the rock once again disappeared below the surf.

After collecting more fish and birds, they sat down for the evening meal. With a dependable source of water and a seemingly bountiful supply of food, they now thought it possible to hold out indefinitely on the island. At the very least, they could stay at Henderson until they had recovered their strength and repaired their worn-out whaleboats for a final attempt at reaching South America. That night they agreed to remain on the island for at least another four or five days before they decided "whether it would be advisable to make any arrangement for a more permanent abode." Their stomachs full and their thirst slaked, they quickly drifted off into what Chase described as a "most comfortable and delicious sleep."

At eleven o'clock the next morning, they returned to the spring. They arrived just as the tide fell below the rock. At first the water was somewhat salty, raising fears that the spring was not as reliable a source of freshwater as they had first thought. But as the tide continued to retreat, the quality of the water steadily improved. After filling their casks with about twenty gallons, they set out in search of food.

Every spare moment of every day was, in Chase's words, "employed in roving about for food." The evening hours proved the most productive, for it was then that the plump white birds known as tropic birds, about the size of chickens, returned to shore to feed their young. Approaching stealthily, the men would "pounce upon [the birds] with a stick and take them without difficulty."

They were not the only ones who lay in wait for the tropic birds each evening. There were also what Nickerson called the man-of-war hawks. But instead of killing the tropic birds, the hawks had what scientists call a kleptoparasitic relationship with them, pecking their backs and beating them with their wings until the tropic birds released the fish that had been intended for their young. With the food in their beaks, the hawks would fly away, "leaving," Nickerson observed, "the young tropic birds supperless."

The following day, December 24, they detected an alarming change. Nickerson noticed that the birds, "being so constantly harassed, began to forsake the island." That evening some of the crew returned to camp complaining that they had not been able to find enough to eat. In just five days, these twenty starving men had exhausted their portion of the island. "Every accessible part of the mountain, contiguous to us, or within the reach of our weak enterprise," Chase wrote, "was already ransacked, for bird's eggs and grass, and was rifled of all that they contained."

➤   ➤   ➤

There was no Christmas feast for the *Essex* crew. That evening they "found that a fruitless search for nourishment had not repaid us the labors of a whole day." Only grass remained, and that was "not much relished," Chase wrote, "without some other food." They began to "entertain serious apprehensions that we should not be able to live long here."

By December 26, their seventh day on Henderson and their thirty-fifth since leaving the wreck, they decided to abandon this used-up island. In Chase's words, their situation was "worse than it would have been in our boats on the ocean; because, in the latter case we should be still making some progress towards the land, while our provisions lasted." In preparation for their departure, they had already begun working on the whaleboats. "We nailed our boats as well as it was possible to do," Nickerson wrote, "with the small quantity of boat nails in our possession, in order to prepare them to stand against the boisterous elements which we were again . . . to encounter."

The coast of Chile was approximately three thousand miles away—about twice as far as they had already sailed. Upon studying their copies of Bowditch's *Navigator*, they realized that Easter Island, at latitude 27°9' south, longitude 109°35' west, was less than a third of that distance. Although they, once again, knew nothing about the island, they decided to sail for it, belatedly realizing that the potential terrors of an unknown island were nothing compared to the known terrors of an open boat in the open ocean.

Early in the day, "all hands were called together," Nickerson remembered, "for a last talk previous to taking a final departure." Pollard explained that they would be leaving the next day and that the boat-crews would remain the same as they'd been prior to their arrival on Henderson. It was then that three men came forward—Joy's boatsteerer Thomas Chappel and two teenagers from Cape Cod, Seth Weeks and William Wright, from Pollard's and Chase's boats, respectively. Several times over the last few days these three white off-islanders had been observed "reasoning upon the probabilities of their deliverance." And the more they talked about it, the more they dreaded the prospect of climbing back into the whaleboats.

Chappel could see that second mate Matthew Joy did not have long to live. As the rest of the crew gradually regained weight and strength during the week on Henderson, Joy, who had possessed a "weak and sickly constitution" even before the sinking, had remained shockingly thin. Chappel knew that if Joy should die, he would become, by default, his whaleboat's leader—a prospect no reasonable man would want, given what might lie ahead.

They had all seen how the man-of-war hawks robbed the tropic birds of their food. As conditions deteriorated on the boats, one could only wonder who of these nine Nantucketers, six African Americans, and five white off-islanders would become the hawks and who would become the tropic birds. Chappel, Wright, and Weeks decided that they did not want to find out.

"The rest of us could make no objection to their plan," Chase wrote, "as it lessened the load of our boats, [and] allowed us their share of the provisions." Even the first mate had to admit that "the probability of their being able to sustain themselves on the island was much stronger than that of our reaching the mainland." Pollard assured the three men that if he did make it back to South America, he would do everything in his power to see that they were rescued.

With downcast eyes and trembling lips, the three men drew away from the rest of the crew. They'd already picked a spot, well removed from the original encampment, on which to construct a crude shelter out of tree branches. It was time they started work.

But their seventeen shipmates were reluctant to see them go, offering "every little article that could be spared from the boats." After accepting the gifts, Chappel and his two companions turned and started down the beach.

> ➤ ➤ ➤

That evening Pollard wrote what he assumed would be his last letter home. It was addressed to his wife, Mary, the twenty-year-old ropemaker's daughter with whom he had spent the sum total of fifty-seven days of married life. He also wrote another, more public letter:

> *Account of the loss of the Ship* Essex *of Nantucket in North America, Ducies Island, December 20, 1820, commanded by Capt. Pollard, jun. which shipwreck happened on the 20th day of November, 1820 on the equator in long. 120° W done by a large whale striking her in the bow, which caused her to fill with water in about 10 minutes. We got what provisions and water the boats would carry, and left her on the 22nd of November, and arrived here this day with all hands, except one black man, who left the ship at Ticamus. We intend to leave tomorrow, which will be the 26th of December [actually December 27], 1820, for the continent. I shall leave with this a letter for my wife, and whoever finds, and will have the goodness to forward it will oblige an unfortunate man, and receive his sincere wishes.*
>
> George Pollard, Jun.

> ➤ ➤ ➤

To the west of their encampment, they had found a large tree with the name of a ship—the *Elizabeth*—carved into it. They placed the letters in a small wooden box they nailed to the trunk.

On December 27 at ten o'clock in the morning, by which time the tide had risen far enough to allow the boats to float over the rocks that surrounded the island, they began to load up. In Pollard's boat were his boatsteerer, Obed Hendricks, along with their fellow Nantucketers Barzillai Ray, Owen Coffin, and Charles Ramsdell, and the African American Samuel Reed. Owen Chase's crew was down to five: the Nantucketers Benjamin Lawrence and Thomas Nickerson, along with Richard Peterson, the elderly black from New York, and Isaac Cole, a young white off-islander. Joy's crew contained the white off-islander Joseph West and four blacks—Lawson Thomas, Charles Shorter, Isaiah Sheppard, and the steward William Bond. Not only were these men under the command of a seriously ill second mate, but Chappel's decision to remain on the island had left them without a boatsteerer to assist Joy in the management of the crew. But neither Pollard nor Chase was willing to part with a Nantucket-born boatsteerer.

Soon it was time for them to leave the island. But Chappel, Wright, and Weeks were nowhere to be found. "[T]hey had not come down," Chase wrote, "either to assist us to get off, nor to take any kind of leave of us." The first mate walked down the beach to their dwelling and told them they were about to set sail. The men were, Chase observed, "very much affected," and one of them began to cry. "They wished us to write to their relations, should Providence safely direct us again to our homes, and said but little else." Seeing that they were "ill at heart about taking any leave of us," Chase bid them a hasty good-bye and left for the boats. "They followed me with their eyes," he wrote, "until I was out of sight, and I never saw more of them."

It had been more of a tease than a salvation, but Henderson Island had at least given them a fighting chance. Back on December 20, Chase had seen "death itself staring us in the face." Now, after more than a week of food and drink, their casks were full of freshwater. Their boats no longer leaked. In addition to hardtack, each crew had some fish and birds. There were also three fewer men to support. "We again set sail," Nickerson wrote, "finally [leaving] this land which had been so providentially thrown in our way."

They are leaving the island

10

THE WHISPER OF NECESSITY

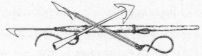

Before they left Henderson Island, Chase loaded a flat stone and an armful of firewood into each boat. That first evening back on the water, as both the island and the sun slipped below the western horizon behind them, they put the stones to use as platforms for cooking fires. "[W]e kept our fires going," Chase wrote, "and cooked our fish and birds, and felt our situation as comfortable as could be expected."

For a month they had been driven south and even west; now they hoped to sail almost directly east to Easter Island. For this to happen they needed two weeks of westerly breezes. However, at latitude 24° south, they were still in the trades, where for more than 70 percent of the year the wind blows out of the southeast. But that night, as if in answer to their prayers, a strong breeze sprang up out of the northwest, and they steered straight for Easter.

If they were to keep track of their progress east, they needed to find a way to estimate their longitude—something they had not done during the first leg of the voyage. A month of sailing without knowing their east-to-west position had proved to them the necessity of at least attempting to determine it. Before leaving Henderson, they decided to maintain what Chase called "a regular reckoning." Their noon observation told them their latitude, and by doing as Captain Bligh had done before them—using an improvised log line to gauge their speed and their compass to determine their direction—they could calculate their longitude. The *Essex* boats were no longer sailing blind.

For three days the northwesterly breeze held. Then, on December 30, the wind shifted into the east-southeast, and for two days they were forced to steer a course well to the south of Easter Island. But by the first day of the new year, 1821, the wind had shifted to the north, and they were once again back on track.

On January 3 they sailed into what Nickerson called "hard weather." Squalls blasted them from the southwest. "The seas had become so rough," Nickerson remembered, "that we were fearful that each successive gust would swamp our boats. . . . Every squall was attended with the most vivid flashes of lightning and awful thunder claps, which seemed to cause the very bosom of the deep to tremble and threw a cheerless aspect upon the face of the ocean."

The next day, the wind shifted to the east-northeast. Pollard and Chase came to the same distressing conclusion: they were now too far to the south to have any hope of reaching the island. They searched their *Navigator* copies for the next closest island "where the wind would allow of our going." About eight hundred miles off the Chilean coast are the islands of Juan Fernandez and Masafuera. Unfortunately there were more than 2,500 miles between them and these islands—farther than they had sailed since leaving the *Essex* forty-four days before.

On the same day that they abandoned all hope of reaching Easter Island, they ate the last of their fish and birds. It was back to their daily ration of a cup of water and three ounces of hardtack per man.

For the next two days, the wind deserted them. The sun beat down with the same force that had so oppressed them prior to their arrival at Henderson. The conditions were the hardest on Matthew Joy, whose bowels had ceased to function. Ever since leaving the island he had continued to deteriorate, and his glassy, distracted eyes had taken on the unmistakable look of death.

On January 7, a breeze rose up out of the north. Their noon observation revealed that they had slipped almost six degrees of latitude, or 360 nautical miles, to the south. But it was their progress to the east that most concerned them. They estimated that they were now only six hundred miles closer to the mainland than when they had left Henderson eleven days before.

The next day Matthew Joy made a request. The twenty-seven-year-old second mate asked if he might be moved to the captain's boat. The transfer was effected, Chase wrote, "under the impression that he would be more comfortable there, and more attention and pains be bestowed in nursing and endeavoring to comfort him." But all knew the real reason for the second mate's removal. Now that he was reaching the end, Joy, who had been on a boat with five off-islanders, wanted to die among his own people.

Joy came from an old Quaker family. Near the town hall on Nantucket his grandfather had owned a large house that was still referred to as the Reuben Joy homestead. In 1800, when Matthew was only seven years old, his parents moved the family to Hudson, New York, where Nantucketers had established a whaling port soon after the Revolution. Matthew remained a Friend until 1817, when he returned to his native island to wed nineteen-year-old Nancy Slade, a Congregationalist. As was customary in such cases, he was disowned that year by the Nantucket Monthly Meeting for "marrying out."

Joy was no longer a Quaker, but on January 10, a hot, windless day in the Pacific, he demonstrated a Friend's sense of duty and devotion. For the last two days his boat-crew had been left leaderless; he now asked to be returned to them. His loyalty to his crew was in the end greater than his need for comfort from his fellow Nantucketers. The transfer was made, and by four o'clock that afternoon Matthew Joy was dead.

Nantucket's Quaker Graveyard was without worldly monuments of any kind, and many had compared its smooth, unmarred sweep to the anonymous surface of the sea. Like that graveyard thousands of miles away, the sea that morning was calm and smooth—not a breath of air ruffled the Pacific's slow, rhythmic swell. The three boats were brought together, and after sewing Joy up in his clothes, they tied a stone to his feet and "consigned him in a solemn manner to the ocean."

Even though they knew Joy had been ill for quite some time, his loss hit them hard. "It was an incident," Chase wrote, "which threw a gloom over our feelings for many days." The last two weeks had been particularly difficult for the men on the second mate's boat. Instead of drawing strength and inspiration from their leader, they had been required to expend valuable energy nursing him. Making it even harder was the absence of Joy's boatsteerer, Thomas Chappel. To fill the void, Pollard ordered his own boatsteerer, the twenty-one-year-old Obed Hendricks, to take command of the second mate's shaken and dispirited crew.

Soon after taking over the steering oar, Hendricks made a disturbing discovery. Joy's illness had apparently prevented him from closely monitoring the distribution of his boat's provisions. As best as Hendricks could determine, there was only enough hardtack in his boat's cuddy to last two, maybe three more days.

>   >   >

Throughout the morning and afternoon of the following day—the fifty-second since the men had left the *Essex*—the wind built out of the northwest until by nightfall it was blowing a full gale. The men took in all sail and steered their boats before the wind. The boats surfed wildly down the crests of the waves. "Flashes of lightning were quick and vivid," Chase wrote, "and the rain came down in cataracts." Instead of being terrified, the men were exhilarated to know that each fifty-knot gust was blowing them toward their destination. "Although the danger was very great," Nickerson remembered, "yet none seemed to dread this so much as death by starvation, and I believe none would have exchanged this terrific gale for a more moderate head wind or a calm."

Visibility was low that night in the driving rain. They had agreed that in the event they became separated, they would steer a course of east-southeast in the hope that they would be within sight of one another come daybreak. As usual, Chase was in the lead. Every minute or so, he turned his head to make sure he could see the other two boats. But at around eleven o'clock he glanced back and saw nothing. "It was blowing and raining at this time as if the heavens were separating," he wrote, "and I knew not hardly at the moment what to do." He decided to head up into the wind and hove to. After drifting for about an hour, "expecting every moment that they would come up with [us]," Chase and his men resumed their agreed-upon course, hopeful that, as had happened before, they would sight the other boats in the morning.

"As soon as daylight appeared," Nickerson wrote, "every man in our boat raised [himself] searching the waters." Grabbing the masts, and one another, for support, they stood up on the seats, craning their necks for a glimpse of their lost companions on the wave-fringed horizon. But they had disappeared. "It was folly to repine at the circumstances," Chase commented; "it could neither be remedied, nor could sorrow secure their return; but it was impossible to prevent ourselves feeling all the poignancy and bitterness that characterizes the separation of men who have long suffered in each other's company, and whose interests and feelings fate had so closely linked together."

They were at latitude 32°16' south, longitude 112°20' west, about six hundred miles south of Easter Island. Nineteen days from Henderson, with more than a thousand miles still left to go, Chase and his men were alone. "For many days after this accident, our progress was attended with dull and melancholy reflections," he wrote. "We had lost the cheering of each other's faces, that, which strange as it is, we so much required in both our mental and bodily distresses."

The squalls and rain continued through the next day. Chase decided to take an inventory of their remaining provisions. Thanks to his rigorous supervision, they still had a considerable store of bread left. But they had been fifty-four days at sea, and there were more than 1,200 miles between them and the island of Juan Fernandez. "Necessity began to whisper [to] us," Chase wrote, "that a still further reduction of our allowance must take place, or we must abandon altogether the hopes of reaching the land, and rely wholly on the chance of being taken up by a vessel."

They were already on half provisions, eating only three ounces of bread a day. "[H]ow to reduce the daily quantity of food, with any regard to life itself, was a question of the utmost consequence." Three ounces of hardtack provided them with only two hundred and fifty calories a day, less than 15 percent of their daily needs. Chase told his men that they had no choice but to cut these half rations once again—to only one and a half ounces of bread a day. This, he knew, "must, in short time, reduce us to mere skeletons again."

It was a terrifying dilemma, and Chase did not arrive at the decision easily. "It required a great effort to bring matters to this dreadful alternative," he wrote. "[E]ither . . . feed our bodies and our hopes a little longer, or in the agonies of hunger to seize upon and devour our provisions, and coolly await the approach of death." Somewhere to the north of them, their companions were about to discover the consequences of taking the latter course.

➤   ➤   ➤

The men in Pollard's and Hendricks's boats were just as gravely affected by the separation. They continued on, however, almost confident that they would once again meet up with Chase's boat. That day, January 14, Obed Hendricks's boat ran out of provisions. For Hendricks and his five crew members—Joseph West, Lawson Thomas, Charles Shorter, Isaiah Sheppard, and William Bond—the question was whether Pollard would be willing to share his boat's provisions.

Having placed Hendricks in command of the second mate's boat only three days before, Pollard could not easily deny his former boat-steerer some of his own stock of food. And if he was willing to feed Hendricks, he would have to feed the other five. So Pollard and his men shared with them what little bread they had, knowing full well that in only a few more days there would be nothing left.

Chase's separation from Pollard and Hendricks saved the first mate from having to face this painful predicament. From the beginning, Chase had strictly, even obsessively, attended to the distribution of rations aboard his boat. To throw open his sea chest of provisions to Hendricks's men, all of them off-islanders who had begun the ordeal with the same amount of bread as his crew, would have been, from Chase's perspective, an act of collective suicide. Earlier in the ordeal the men had discussed the possibility of having to share their provisions if one of the crews should lose their stock. "[S]uch a course of conduct," Chase wrote, "was calculated to weaken the chances of a final deliverance for some, and might be the only means of con-signing every soul of us to a horrid death of starvation." For Chase, intent on getting himself and his boat-crew to safety, no matter what, the separation from Pollard's and Hendricks's boats could not have been better timed.

On the same day that Chase cut his crew's daily ration of bread in half, the wind gradually died to nothing. The clouds thinned until the sun's rays once again became overwhelming. In desperation, Chase and his men tore the sails from the spars and hid beneath the salt-encrusted canvas. Swaddling themselves in the sails, they lay down in the bottom of the boat and "abandoned her," the first mate wrote, "to the mercy of the waves."

Despite the severity of the sun, the men did not complain of thirst. After a week of drinking their fill at Henderson Island, they had been rehydrated to the extent that food had replaced water as their most desperate need. In fact some of the men were now suffering from diarrhea—a common symptom of starvation—which Chase attributed to the "relaxing effects of the water." As he put it, "we were fast wasting away."

While the body can rebound quite quickly from dehydration, it takes a frustratingly long time to recover from the effects of starvation. The *Essex* crew's week on Henderson did little to restore their bodies' reserves of muscle and fat. Now, three weeks later, the sailors were as close to starving to death as they'd ever been.

Chase reported that they barely had the strength "to move about in our boats, and slowly perform the necessary labors appertaining to [them]." That evening, when they sat up from the bottom of the boat, they experienced blackouts. "Upon [our] attempting to rise again," Chase wrote, "the blood would rush into the head, and an intoxicating blindness come over us, almost to occasion our suddenly falling down again."

Chase's sufferings were so severe that he forgot to lock the lid of his sea chest before falling asleep in the bottom of the boat. That night one of the crew awoke the first mate and informed him that Richard Peterson, the old black man from New York who had led them all in prayer, had stolen some bread.

Chase leaped up in a rage. "I felt at the moment the highest indignation and resentment at such conduct in any of our crew," he wrote, "and immediately took my pistol in my hand, and charged him if he had taken any [bread], to give it up without the least hesitation, or I should instantly shoot him!" Peterson quickly returned the provisions, "pleading," Chase wrote, "the hard necessity that urged him to do it." Almost three times the age of anyone else in the boat, Peterson was reaching the end of his endurance, and he knew that without more bread, he would soon die.

Nonetheless, the first mate felt that an example had to be made. "This was the first infraction," he wrote, "and the security of our lives, our hopes of redemption from our sufferings, loudly called for a prompt and signal punishment." But, as Nickerson observed, Peterson "was a good old man, and nothing but the cravings of a starved appetite could have induced him to be guilty of so rash an attempt." Chase finally decided to grant him mercy. "I could not find it in my soul to extend towards him the least severity on this account," he wrote, "however much, according to the strict imposition which we felt upon ourselves it might demand." Chase warned Peterson that if he attempted to steal again, it would cost him his life.

Light breezes persisted throughout the next day and into the following night. The tensions among Chase's crew had begun to ease, but their individual suffering continued unabated, their bodies wracked by a hunger that the daily ration of an ounce and a half of bread hardly began to alleviate. Still, the distribution of provisions remained the most important part of the day. Some of the men attempted to make their portion last as long as possible, nibbling it almost daintily and savoring each tiny morsel with what little saliva their mouths could generate. Others ate their ration virtually whole, hoping to provide their stomachs with at least some sensation of fullness. Afterward, all of them carefully licked the residue from their fingers.

That night the placid waters around Chase's boat suddenly erupted into pale foam as something enormous slammed into the stern. Clinging to the gunwales, the men rose up from the bottom of the boat and saw that a shark, nearly as large as the killer whale that had attacked Pollard's boat, was "swimming about us in a most ravenous manner, making attempts every now and then upon different parts of the boat, as if he would devour the very wood." The monster snapped at the steering oar, then tried to get its massive jaws around the boat's sternpost, as if possessed by the same gnawing hunger that was consuming all of them.

In the bottom of the boat was a lance just like the one Chase had been tempted to hurl at the whale that sank the *Essex*. If they could kill this giant shark, they'd have enough food to last them for several weeks. But when Chase attempted to stab the creature, he discovered that he did not have the strength even to dent its sandpaper-like skin. "[H]e was so much larger than an ordinary [shark]," Chase wrote, "and manifested such a fearless malignity, as to make us afraid of him; and our utmost efforts, which were at first directed to kill him for prey, became in the end self-defense." There was little the men could do as the shark pushed and slapped their whaleboat's thin sides. Eventually, the shark grew bored with them. "Baffled . . . in all his hungry attempts upon us," Chase wrote, "he shortly made off."

The next day a group of porpoises replaced the shark. For almost an hour Chase's men did everything they could to catch one of these playful creatures. Whenever a porpoise surfaced near the boat, they tried to stab it with the lance. But as had been true with the shark, they could not, in Nickerson's words, "muster strength sufficient to pierce through their tough hide." While a shark is a primitive killing machine, a porpoise is one of the most intelligent mammals on earth. The porpoises' mastery of their environment was now cruelly obvious to this boatload of starving land-dwellers. "[T]hey soon left us," Nickerson wrote, "apparently in high glee[,] leaping from the water and . . . in full exercise of every enjoyment. Poor devils, how much they are now our superiors and yet not . . . know it."

For the next two days, January 17 and 18, the calms returned. "[T]he distresses of a cheerless prospect and a burning hot sun were," Chase wrote, "once again visited upon our devoted heads." As they approached their sixtieth day since leaving the *Essex*, even Chase had become convinced that it was their destiny to die. "We began to think that Divine Providence had abandoned us at last," the first mate wrote, "and it was but an unavailing effort to endeavor to prolong a now tedious existence." They could not help but wonder *how* they would die: "Horrible were the feelings that took possession of us!—The contemplation of a death of agony and torment, refined by the most dreadful and distressing reflections, absolutely prostrated both body and soul."

Chase called the night of January 18 "a despairing era in our sufferings." Two months of deprivation and fear had reached an unbearable climax as they anticipated the horrors to come. "[O]ur minds were wrought up to the highest pitch of dread and apprehension for our fate," Chase wrote, "and all in them was dark, gloomy, and confused."

At around eight o'clock, the darkness came to life with a familiar sound: the breathing of sperm whales. It was a black night, and the noise that had once signaled the thrill of the hunt now terrified them. "[W]e could distinctly hear the furious thrashing of their tails in the water," Chase remembered, "and our weak minds pictured out their appalling and hideous aspects."

As the whales surfaced and dove around them, Richard Peterson "took an immediate fright" and pleaded with his companions to row them to safety. But no one had the strength even to lift an oar. After three whales passed the stern in rapid succession, "blowing and spouting at a terrible rate," the pod disappeared.

When Peterson's panic had receded, he talked with Chase about his religious beliefs. Although he knew his own death was imminent, Peterson's faith in God remained undiminished. "[H]e reasoned very sensibly," Chase wrote, "and with much composure." Peterson had a wife back in New York City, and he asked Chase to contact her if the first mate should ever reach home alive.

The next day, January 19, the wind blew so fiercely that they had to take in their sails and lie to. Lightning flashed and the rain poured down as the wind shifted through "every point of the compass." As their little craft tossed in the confused seas, Peterson lay between the seats of the boat, "utterly dispirited and broken down." That evening the wind finally settled into the east-northeast.

On January 20, exactly two months since the sinking of the *Essex*, Richard Peterson declared that it was his time to die. When Chase offered Peterson his daily ration of bread, he refused it, saying, "It may be of service to someone but can be of none to me." Soon after, he lost the power of speech.

Modern-day proponents of euthanasia have long endorsed the combined effects of starvation and dehydration as a painless and dignified way for a terminally ill patient to die. In the final stages, hunger pangs cease, as does the sensation of thirst. The patient slips into unconsciousness as the deterioration of his internal organs results in a peaceful death. This was apparently how Richard Peterson passed away. "[T]he breath appeared to be leaving his body without the least pain," Chase reported, "and at four o'clock he was gone."

The next day, at latitude 35°07' south, longitude 105°46' west, a thousand miles from Juan Fernandez Island, Peterson's body joined Joy's in the vast burial ground of the sea.

11

GAMES OF CHANCE

On January 20, 1821, eight days after losing sight of Chase's boat, Pollard's and Hendricks's men were coming to the end of their provisions. That day, Lawson Thomas, one of the blacks on Hendricks's boat, died. With barely a pound of hardtack left to share among ten men, Hendricks and his crew dared speak of a subject that had been on all their minds: whether they should eat, instead of bury, the body.

For as long as men had been sailing the world's oceans, famished sailors had been sustaining themselves on the remains of dead shipmates. By the early nineteenth century, cannibalism at sea was so widespread that survivors often felt compelled to inform their rescuers if they had *not* resorted to it since, according to one historian, "suspicion of this practice among starving castaways was a routine reaction."

Two months after deciding to spurn the Society Islands because, in Pollard's words, "we feared we should be devoured by cannibals," the men of the *Essex* were about to eat one of their own shipmates.

First they had to butcher the body. On Nantucket there was a slaughterhouse at the foot of Old North Wharf where any island boy could watch a cow or sheep be transformed into marketable cuts of meat. On a whaleship it was the black members of the crew who prepared and cooked the food. In the case of the *Essex*, more than thirty hogs and dozens of tortoises had been butchered by the African American cook before the whale attack. And, of course, all twenty crew members had taken part in the cutting up of several dozen sperm whales. But this was not a whale or a hog or a tortoise. This was Lawson Thomas, a shipmate with whom they had shared two hellish months in an open boat. Whoever butchered Thomas's body had to contend not only with the cramped quarters of a twenty-five-foot boat but also with the chaos of his own emotions.

Instead of easing their hunger pangs, their first taste of meat only intensified their urge to eat. The saliva flowed in their mouths as their awakened stomachs gurgled with digestive juices. And the more they ate, the hungrier they became.

Anthropologists and archaeologists studying the phenomenon of cannibalism have estimated that the average human adult would provide about sixty-six pounds of edible meat. But Lawson Thomas's body was not average. Autopsies of starvation victims have revealed a dramatic atrophy of muscle tissue and a complete absence of fat. Starvation and dehydration had also shrunk Thomas's internal organs, including the heart and liver. His body may have yielded as little as thirty pounds of lean, stringy meat. On the following day, when the captain's store of bread ran out, Pollard and his men "were glad to partake of the wretched fare with the other crew."

Two days later, on January 23—the sixty-third day since leaving the wreck—yet another member of Hendricks's crew died and was eaten. And like Lawson Thomas before him, Charles Shorter was black.

➤   ➤   ➤

More than a hundred miles to the south, as their shipmates consumed their second body in four days, Owen Chase and his men drifted in a windless sea. A week of eating only one and a half ounces of bread a day had left them "hardly able to crawl around the boat, and possessing but strength enough to convey our scanty morsel to our mouths." Boils had begun to break out on their skin. On the morning of January 24, with another day of calms and broiling sun ahead of them, Chase was certain that some of his crew would not see nightfall. "[W]hat it was that buoyed me above all the terrors which surrounded us," Chase wrote, "God alone knows."

That night, the first mate had a vivid dream. He had just sat down to a "splendid and rich repast, where there was everything that the most dainty appetite could desire." But just as he reached for his first taste of food, he "awoke to the cold realities of my miserable situation." Fired to a kind of madness by his dream, Chase began to gnaw on the leather sheathing of an oar only to find that he lacked the strength in his jaws to penetrate the stiff, salt-caked hide.

With the death of Peterson, Chase's crew had been whittled down to only three—Nantucketers Benjamin Lawrence and Thomas Nickerson, along with Isaac Cole from Rochester, Massachusetts. As their sufferings mounted, the men relied increasingly on the first mate. Chase reported that they "press[ed] me continually with questions upon the probability of our reaching land again. I kept constantly rallying my spirits to enable me to afford them comfort."

Chase had changed since the beginning of the ordeal. Instead of the harsh disciplinarian who had doled out rations with a gun by his side, he now spoke to the men in what Nickerson described as an almost cheerful voice. As their torments reached new heights, Chase recognized that it wasn't discipline his men needed but encouragement. For as they had all seen with Peterson, hope was all that stood between them and death.

Nickerson called the first mate a "remarkable man" and recognized Chase's genius for identifying hope in a seemingly hopeless situation. Having already endured so much, Chase reasoned, they owed it to one another to cling as stubbornly to life as possible: "I reasoned with them, and told them that we would not die sooner by keeping our hopes." But it was more than a question of loyalty to one another. As far as Chase was concerned, God was also involved in this struggle for survival. "[T]he dreadful sacrifices and privations we [had] endured were to preserve us from death," he assured them, "and were not to be put in competition with the price which we set upon our lives." In addition to saying it would be "unmanly to repine at what neither admitted of alleviation nor cure," Chase insisted that "it was our solemn duty to recognize in our calamities an overruling divinity, by whose mercy we might be suddenly snatched from peril, and to rely upon him alone, 'Who tempers the wind to the shorn lamb.' " Although they had seen little evidence of the Lord's mercy in the last two months, Chase insisted that they "bear up against all evils . . . and not weakly distrust the providence of the Almighty, by giving ourselves up to despair."

For the next three days the wind continued out of the east, forcing them farther and farther south. "[I]t was impossible to silence the rebellious repinings of our nature," Chase admitted. "It was our cruel lot not to have had one bright anticipation realized—not one wish of our thirsting souls gratified."

On January 26, the sixty-sixth day since leaving the wreck, their noon observation indicated that they had sunk to latitude 36° south, more than 600 nautical miles south of Henderson Island and 1,800 miles due west of Valparaiso, Chile. That day the searing sun gave way to a bitterly cold rain. Starvation had lowered their body temperatures by several degrees, and with few clothes to warm their thin bodies, they were now in danger of dying of hypothermia. They had no choice but to try to head north, back toward the equator.

With the breeze out of the east, they were forced to tack, turning with the steering oar until the wind came from the starboard side of the boat. Prior to reaching Henderson, it had been a maneuver they had accomplished with ease. Now, even though the wind was quite light, they no longer had the strength to handle the steering oar or trim the sails. "[A]fter much labor, we got our boat about," Chase remembered, "and so great was the fatigue attending this small exertion of our bodies, that we all gave up for a moment and abandoned her to her own course."

With no one steering or adjusting the sails, the boat drifted aimlessly. The men lay helpless and shivering in the bilge as, Chase wrote, "the horrors of our situation came upon us with a despairing force and effect." After two hours, they finally marshaled enough strength to adjust the sails so that the boat was once again moving forward. But now they were sailing north, parallel to, but not toward, the coast of South America. Like Job before him, Chase could not help but ask, "[What] narrow hopes [still] bound us to life?"

➤　➤　➤

As Chase's men lay immobilized by hunger in the bottom of their boat, yet another member of Hendricks's crew died. This time it was Isaiah Sheppard, who became the third African American to die and be eaten in only seven days. The next day, January 28—the sixty-eighth day since leaving the wreck—Samuel Reed, the sole black member of Pollard's crew, died and was eaten. That left William Bond in Hendricks's boat as the last surviving black in the *Essex*'s crew. There was little doubt who had become the tropic birds and who had become the hawks.

Given the cruel mathematics of survival cannibalism, each death not only provided the remaining men with food but reduced by one the number of people they had to share it with. By the time Samuel Reed died on January 28, the seven survivors each received close to three thousand calories' worth of meat (up by almost a third since the death of Lawson Thomas). Unfortunately, even though this portion may have been roughly equivalent to each man's share of a Galapagos tortoise, it lacked the fat that the human body requires to digest meat. No matter how much meat they now had available to them, it was of limited nutritional value without a source of fat.

The following night, January 29, was darker than most. The two boat-crews were finding it difficult to keep track of each other; they also lacked the strength to manage the steering oars and sails. That night, Pollard and his men looked up to find that the whaleboat containing Obed Hendricks, William Bond, and Joseph West had disappeared. Pollard's men were too weak to attempt to find the missing boat—either by raising a lantern or firing a pistol. That left George Pollard, Owen Coffin, Charles Ramsdell, and Barzillai Ray—all Nantucketers—alone for the first time since the sinking of the *Essex*. They were at latitude 35° south, longitude 100° west, 1,500 miles from the coast of South America, with only the half-eaten corpse of Samuel Reed to keep them alive.

But no matter how grim their prospects might seem, they were better than those of Hendricks's boat-crew. Without a compass or a quadrant, Hendricks and his men were now lost in an empty and limitless sea.

➤   ➤   ➤

On February 6, the four men on Pollard's boat, having consumed "the last morsel" of Samuel Reed, began to "[look] at each other with horrid thoughts in our minds," according to one survivor, "but we held our tongues." Then the youngest of them, sixteen-year-old Charles Ramsdell, uttered the unspeakable. They should cast lots, he said, to see who would be killed so that the rest could live.

The drawing of lots in a survival situation had long been an accepted custom of the sea. The earliest recorded instance dates back to the first half of the seventeenth century, when seven Englishmen sailing from the Caribbean island of St. Kitts were driven out to sea in a storm. After seventeen days, one of the crew suggested that they cast lots. As it turned out, the lot fell to the man who had originally made the proposal, and after lots were cast again to see who should execute him, he was killed and eaten.

When first presented with young Ramsdell's proposal, Captain Pollard "would not listen to it," according to an account related by Nickerson, "saying to the others, 'No, but if I die first you are welcome to subsist on my remains.' " Then Owen Coffin, Pollard's first cousin, the eighteen-year-old son of his aunt, joined Ramsdell in requesting that they cast lots.

Pollard studied his three young companions. Starvation had ringed their sunken eyes with a dark, smudgelike pigmentation. There was little doubt that they were all close to death. It was also clear that all of them, including Barzillai Ray, the orphaned son of a noted island cooper, were in favor of Ramsdell's proposal. As he had two times before—after the knockdown in the Gulf Stream and the sinking of the *Essex*—Pollard acquiesced to the majority. He agreed to cast lots. If suffering had turned Chase into a compassionate yet forceful leader, Pollard's confidence had been eroded even further by events that reduced him to the most desperate extreme a man can ever know.

They cut up a scrap of paper and placed the pieces in a hat. The lot fell to Owen Coffin. "My lad, my lad!" Pollard cried out. "[I]f you don't like your lot, I'll shoot the first man that touches you." Then the captain offered to take the lot himself. "Who can doubt but that Pollard would rather have met the death a thousand times," Nickerson wrote. "None that knew him, will ever doubt."

But Coffin had already resigned himself to his fate. "I like it as well as any other," he said softly.

Lots were drawn again to see who would shoot the boy. It fell to Coffin's friend Charles Ramsdell.

Even though the lottery had originally been his idea, Ramsdell now refused to follow it through. "For a long time," Nickerson wrote, "he declared that he could never do it, but finally had to submit." Before he died, Coffin spoke a parting message to his mother, which

owen coffen had died

Pollard promised to deliver if he should make it back to Nantucket. Then Coffin asked for a few moments of silence. After reassuring the others that "the lots had been fairly drawn," he laid his head down on the boat's gunwale. "He was soon dispatched," Pollard would later recall, "and nothing of him left."

A lot of people are dieing! They also are eating each other

12

IN THE EAGLE'S SHADOW

Chase and his men lay in the bottom of their boat in a cold drizzle. All they had to shield them from the rain was a piece of tattered, water-soaked canvas. "Even had it been dry," Nickerson wrote, "[it] would have been but a poor apology for covering."

On January 28, 1821, the breeze finally shifted into the west. But it brought them little comfort. "It had nearly become indifferent to us," Chase wrote, "from what quarter it blew." They now had too far to go and too few provisions to have any hope of reaching land. Their only chance was to be sighted by a ship. "[I]t was this narrow hope alone," Chase remembered, "that prevented me from lying down at once to die."

They had fourteen days of hardtack left, but that assumed they could live two more weeks on only an ounce and a half a day. "We were so feeble," Nickerson wrote, "that we could scarcely crawl about the boat upon our hands and knees." Chase realized that if he didn't increase their daily portion of bread, they all might be dead in as few as five days. It was time to abandon the strict rationing regime that had brought them this far and let the men eat "as pinching necessity demanded."

Success in a long-term survival situation requires that a person display an "active-passive" approach to the gradual and agonizing unfolding of events. "The key factor . . . [is] the realization that passivity is itself a deliberate and 'active' act," the survival psychologist John Leach writes. "There is strength in passivity." After more than two months of regimenting every aspect of his men's lives, Chase intuitively understood this—that it was now time to give "ourselves wholly up to the guidance and disposal of our Creator." They would eat as much bread as they needed to stave off death and see where the westerly wind took them.

By February 6 they were still alive, but just barely. "Our sufferings were now drawing to a close," the first mate wrote. "[A] terrible death appeared shortly to await us." The slight increase in food intake had brought a return to their hunger pangs, which were now "violent and outrageous." They found it difficult to talk and think clearly. Dreams of food and drink continued to torment them. "[O]ften did our fevered minds wander to the side of some richly supplied table," Nickerson remembered. His fantasies always ended the same way—with him "crying at the disappointment."

That night, rain squalls forced them to shorten sail. The off-islander Isaac Cole was on watch, and rather than awaken his companions, he attempted to lower the jib himself. But it proved too much for him. Chase and Nickerson awoke the next morning to find Cole despondent in the bilge of the boat. He declared that "all was dark in his mind, not a single ray of hope was left for him to dwell upon." Like Richard Peterson before him, he had given up, asserting that "it was folly and madness to be struggling against what appeared so palpably to be our fixed and settled destiny."

Even though he barely had the strength to articulate the words, Chase did his best to change Cole's mind. "I remonstrated with him as effectually as the weakness both of my body and understanding would allow of." Suddenly Cole sat up and crawled to the bow and hoisted the jib he had lowered, at such cost, the night before. He cried out that he would not give up and that he would live as long as any of them. "[T]his effort was," Chase wrote, "but the hectic fever of the moment." Cole soon returned to the bottom of the boat, where he lay despairing for the rest of the day and through the night. But Cole would not be permitted the dignity of a quiet and peaceful death.

On the morning of February 8, the seventy-ninth day since leaving the *Essex*, Cole began to rant incoherently, presenting to his frightened crew members "a most miserable spectacle of madness." Twitching spasmodically, he sat up and called for a napkin and water, then fell down to the bottom of the boat as if struck dead, only to pop up again like a possessed jack-in-the-box. By ten o'clock he could no longer speak. Chase and the others placed him on a board they had laid across the seats and covered him with a few pieces of clothing.

For the next six hours, Cole whimpered and moaned in pain, finally falling into "the most horrid and frightful convulsions" Chase had ever seen. In addition to dehydration and hypernatremia (an excess amount of salt), he may have been suffering from a lack of magnesium, a mineral deficiency that, when extreme, can cause bizarre and violent behavior. By four o'clock in the afternoon, Isaac Cole was dead.

It had been forty-three days since they'd left Henderson Island, seventy-eight days since they'd last seen the *Essex*, but no one suggested—at least that afternoon—that they use Cole's body for food. All night the corpse lay beside them, each man keeping his thoughts to himself.

The next morning, February 9, Lawrence and Nickerson began making preparations for burying Cole's remains. Chase stopped them. All night he had wrestled with the question of what they should do. With only three days of hardtack left, he knew, it was quite possible that they might be reduced to casting lots. Better to eat a dead shipmate—even a tainted shipmate—than be forced to kill a man.

"I addressed them," Chase wrote, "on the painful subject of keeping the body for food." Lawrence and Nickerson raised no objections and, fearful that the meat had already begun to spoil, "[we] set to work as fast as we were able."

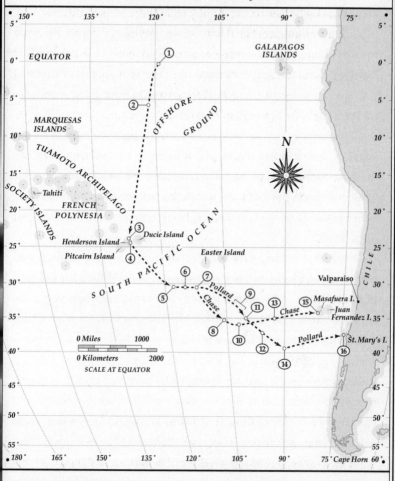

VOYAGES OF THE *ESSEX* WHALEBOATS
November 20, 1820, to February 23, 1821

1/ *Essex* rammed by a whale, November 20, 1820
2/ Pollard's boat attacked by killer whale, November 28
3/ Sight Henderson Island, December 20
4/ Leave Henderson Island, December 27
5/ January 7
6/ Joy dies, January 10
7/ Chase separates from Pollard and Hendricks, January 12
8/ Peterson dies, January 20
9/ Deaths of Thomas, Shorter, Sheppard, and Reed, January 20–28
10/ Chase tacks and heads north, January 26
11/ Pollard and Hendricks separate, January 29
12/ Execution of Coffin, February 6
13/ Death of Cole, February 8
14/ Death of Ray, February 11
15/ Chase rescued, February 18
16/ Pollard rescued, February 23

© 1999 Jeffrey L. Ward

After separating the limbs from the body and removing the heart, they sewed up what remained of Cole's body "as decently" as they could, before they committed it to the sea. Then they began to eat. Even before lighting a fire, the men "eagerly devoured" the heart, then ate "sparingly of a few pieces of the flesh." They cut the rest of the meat into thin strips—some of which they roasted on the fire, while the others were laid out to dry in the sun.

Chase insisted that he had "no language to paint the anguish of our souls in this dreadful dilemma." Making it all the worse was the thought that any one of the remaining three men might be next. "We knew not then," the first mate wrote, "to whose lot it would fall next, either to die or be shot, and eaten like the poor wretch we had just dispatched."

The next morning they discovered that the strips of flesh had turned a rancid green. They immediately cooked the strips, which provided them with enough meat to last another six or seven days, allowing them to save what little bread they had left for what Chase called "the last moment of our trial."

➤   ➤   ➤

In Captain Pollard's boat, on February 11, only five days after the execution of Owen Coffin, Barzillai Ray died. Ray, whose biblical first name means "made of iron, most firm and true," was nineteen years old. It was the seventh death George Pollard and Charles Ramsdell had witnessed in the month and a half since departing Henderson Island.

Psychologists studying the phenomenon of battle fatigue during World War II discovered that no soldiers—regardless of how strong their emotional makeup might be—were able to function if their unit experienced losses of 75 percent or more. Pollard and Ramsdell were suffering from a double burden; not only had they seen seven of nine men die (and even killed one of them), but they had been forced to eat their bodies. Like Pip, the black sailor in *Moby-Dick* who loses his mind after several hours of treading water on a boundless sea, Pollard and Ramsdell had been "carried down alive to the wondrous depths, where strange shapes of the unwarped primal world glided to and fro." Now they were alone, with only the corpse of Barzillai Ray and the bones of Coffin and Reed to sustain them.

Three days later, on February 14, the eighty-fifth day since leaving the wreck, Owen Chase, Benjamin Lawrence, and Thomas Nickerson ate the last of Isaac Cole. A week of living off human flesh, combined with their earlier decision to increase their daily ration of hardtack, had strengthened them to the point where they could once again manage the steering oar. But if they were stronger, they were also in a great deal of pain. As if the boils that covered their skin weren't enough, their arms and legs started to swell shockingly. Known as edema, this accumulation of fluid is a common symptom of starvation.

Several days of westerly winds had brought them to within three hundred miles of the islands of Masafuera and Juan Fernandez. If they averaged sixty miles a day, they might reach safety in another five days. Unfortunately, they had only three days of hardtack left.

"Matters were now with us at their height," Chase wrote. "[A]ll hope was cast upon the breeze; and we tremblingly and fearfully awaited its progress, and the dreadful development of our destiny." Surrendering all prospects, the men were convinced that after two and a half months of suffering they were about to die nearly within sight of salvation.

That night Owen Chase lay down to sleep, "almost indifferent whether I should ever see the light again." He dreamed he saw a ship, just a few miles away, and even though he "strained every nerve to get to her," she sailed off into the distance, never to return. Chase awoke "almost overpowered with the frenzy I had caught in my slumbers, and stung with the cruelties of a diseased and disappointed imagination."

The next afternoon, Chase saw a thick cloud to the northeast—a sure sign of land. It must be the island of Masafuera—at least that was what Chase told Lawrence and Nickerson. In two days, he assured them, they would be on dry land. At first, his companions were reluctant to believe him. Gradually, however, after "repeated assurances of the favorable appearances of things" on the part of Chase, "their spirits acquired even a degree of elasticity that was truly astonishing." The wind remained favorable all night, and with their sails trimmed perfectly and a man tending the steering oar, their little boat made the best time of the voyage.

The next morning the cloud still loomed ahead. The end of their ordeal was apparently only days away. But for fifteen-year-old Thomas Nickerson, the strain of anticipation had become too much. After bailing out the boat, he lay down, drew the mildewed piece of canvas over him like a shroud, and told his fellow crew members that "he wished to die immediately."

"I saw that he had given up," Chase wrote, "and I attempted to speak a few words of comfort and encouragement to him." But all the arguments that had served the first mate so well failed to penetrate Nickerson's inner gloom. "A fixed look of settled and forsaken despondency came over his face," Chase wrote. "[H]e lay for some time silent, sullen, and sorrowful—and I felt at once . . . that the coldness of death was fast gathering upon him."

It was obvious to Chase that some form of dementia had seized the boy. Having watched Isaac Cole slip into a similar madness, Chase could not help but wonder if all of them were about to succumb to the temptations of despair. "[T]here was a sudden and unaccountable earnestness in his manner," he wrote, "that alarmed me, and made me fear that I myself might unexpectedly be overtaken by a like weakness, or dizziness of nature, that would bereave me at once of both reason and life." Whether or not it had been communicated to him through

Cole's diseased flesh, Chase also felt the stirrings of a death wish as dark as the pillarlike cloud ahead.

At seven o'clock the next morning, February 18, Chase was sleeping in the bottom of the boat. Benjamin Lawrence was standing at the steering oar. Throughout the ordeal, the twenty-one-year-old boat-steerer had demonstrated remarkable fortitude. He was the one who, two months earlier, had volunteered to swim underneath the boat to repair a sprung plank. As Lawrence had watched Peterson, Cole, and now Nickerson lose their grip on life, he had clung, as best he could, to hope.

Safe in Lawrence's pocket was the piece of twine he had been working on ever since they'd left the wreck. It was now close to twelve inches long. He leaned into the steering oar and scanned the horizon.

"There's a sail!" he cried.

Chase immediately scrambled to his feet. Just visible over the horizon was the speck of pale brown that Lawrence had taken for a sail. Chase stared for several suspenseful moments, gradually realizing that, yes, it was a sail—the topgallant of a ship, about seven miles away.

"I do not believe it is possible," Chase wrote, "to form a just conception of the pure, strong feelings, and the unmingled emotions of joy and gratitude, that took possession of my mind on this occasion."

Soon even Nickerson was up on his feet and gazing excitedly ahead.

Now the question was whether they could catch up to the much larger vessel. The ship was several miles to leeward, which was an advantage for the smaller vessel, and heading slightly north of their position, which meant that it might intercept their line of sail. Could their whaleboat reach that crossing point at approximately the same time the ship did? Chase could only pray that his nightmare of the missed rescue ship would not prove true. "I felt at the moment," Chase wrote, "a violent and unaccountable impulse to fly directly towards her."

For the next three hours they were in a desperate race. Their battered old whaleboat skimmed lightly over the waves at between four and six knots in the northwesterly breeze. Up ahead, the ship's sail plan continued to emerge from the distant horizon, revealing, with excruciating slowness, not only the topgallant sails but the topsails beneath and, finally, the mainsail and foresail. Yes, they assured themselves, they were catching up to the ship.

There was no lookout at the vessel's masthead, but eventually someone on deck saw them approaching to windward and behind. Chase and his men watched in tense fascination as the antlike figures bustled about the ship, shortening sail. Gradually the whaleboat closed the distance, and the hull of the merchantman rose up out of the sea, looming larger and larger ahead of them until Chase could read her name. She was the *Indian* from London.

Chase heard a shout and through glazed, reddened eyes saw a figure at the quarterdeck rail with a trumpet, a hailing device resembling a megaphone. It was an officer of the *Indian*, asking who they were. Chase summoned all his strength to make himself heard, but his swollen tongue stumbled over the words: "*Essex* . . . whaleship . . . Nantucket."

➤   ➤   ➤

The narratives of shipwreck survivors are filled with accounts of captains refusing to take castaways aboard. In some instances the officers were reluctant to share their already low supply of provisions; in others they were fearful the survivors might be suffering from communicable diseases. But as soon as Chase explained that they were from a wreck, the *Indian*'s captain immediately insisted that they come alongside.

When Chase, Lawrence, and Nickerson attempted to climb aboard, they discovered that they didn't have the strength. The three men stared up at the crew, their eyes wide and huge within the dark hollows of their skulls. Their raw, ulcerated skin hung from their skeletons like noxious rags. As he looked down from the quarterdeck, Captain William Crozier was moved to tears at what Chase called "the most deplorable and affecting picture of suffering and misery."

The English sailors lifted the men from their boat and carried them to the captain's cabin. Crozier ordered the cook to serve them their first taste of civilized food—tapioca pudding. Made from the root of the cassava plant, tapioca is a high-calorie, easy-to-digest food rich in the proteins and carbohydrates that their bodies craved.

Rescue came at latitude 33°45' south, longitude 81°03' west. It was the eighty-ninth day since Chase and his men had left the *Essex*, and at noon they came within sight of Masafuera. Chase had succeeded in navigating them across a 2,500-mile stretch of ocean with astonishing accuracy. Even though they had sometimes been so weak that they could not steer their boat, they had somehow managed to sail almost to within sight of their intended destination. In just a few days the *Indian* would be in the Chilean port of Valparaiso.

Trailing behind on a towline was the whaleboat that had served the Nantucketers so well. Captain Crozier hoped to sell the old boat in Valparaiso and establish a fund for the men's relief. But the next night the weather blew up to a gale, and the boat, empty of men for the first time in three months, was lost.

➤ ➤ ➤

Three hundred miles to the south, Pollard and Ramsdell sailed on. For the next five days they pushed east, until by February 23, the ninety-fourth day since leaving the wreck, they were approaching the island of St. Mary's just off the Chilean coast. Over a year before, this had been the *Essex*'s first landfall after rounding Cape Horn. Pollard and Ramsdell were on the verge of completing an irregular circle with a diameter of more than three thousand miles.

It had been twelve days since the death of Barzillai Ray. They had long since eaten the last scrap of his flesh. The two famished men now cracked open the bones of their shipmates—beating them against the stone on the bottom of the boat and smashing them with the boat's hatchet—and ate the marrow, which contained the fat their bodies so desperately needed.

Pollard would later remember these as "days of horror and despair." Both of them were so weak that they could barely lift their hands. They were drifting in and out of consciousness. It is not uncommon for castaways who have been many days at sea and suffered both physically and emotionally to lapse into what has been called "a sort of collective confabulation," in which the survivors exist in a shared fantasy world. Delusions may include comforting scenes from home—perhaps, in the case of Pollard and Ramsdell, a sunny June day on the Nantucket Commons during the sheepshearing festival. Survivors may find themselves in conversation with deceased shipmates and family members as they lose all sense of time.

For Pollard and Ramsdell, it was the bones—gifts from the men they had known and loved—that became their obsession. They stuffed their pockets with finger bones; they sucked the sweet marrow from the splintered ribs and thighs. And they sailed on, the compass card wavering toward east.

Suddenly they heard a sound: men shouting and then silence as shadows fell across them and then the rustle of wind in sails and the creaking of spars and rigging. They looked up, and there were faces.

➤   ➤   ➤

Of the *Dauphin*'s twenty-one-man crew, at least three—Dimon Peters, Asnonkeets, and Joseph Squibb—were Wampanoags from Cape Cod and Martha's Vineyard. As children they had been taught a legend about the discovery of Nantucket that told of how, long before the arrival of the Europeans, a huge eagle appeared over a village on Cape

Cod. The eagle would swoop down out of the sky and carry off children in its talons, then disappear over the waters to the south. Finally the villagers asked a benevolent giant named Maushop to find out where the eagle was taking their children. Maushop set off to the south, wading through the water until he came to an island he had never seen before. After searching all over the island, he found the bones of the children piled high beneath a large tree.

On the morning of February 23, the crew of the *Dauphin* made a similar discovery. Looking down from their ship, they saw two men in a whaleboat filled with bones.

The men were not much more than skeletons themselves, and the story that would be passed from ship to ship in the months ahead was that they were "found sucking the bones of their dead mess mates, which they were loath to part with." The *Dauphin*'s captain, Zimri Coffin, ordered his men to lower a boat and bring the two survivors aboard. Like Chase, Lawrence, and Nickerson before them, Pollard and Ramsdell were too weak to stand and had to be lifted up to the whaleship's deck. Both men were, in the words of a witness, "very low" when first brought aboard. But after being given some food, Pollard made an astonishing recovery.

At around five o'clock that evening, the *Dauphin* spoke the whaleship *Diana* from New York. The *Diana*'s captain, Aaron Paddack, toward the end of a successful voyage, joined Captain Coffin for dinner. Also joining them was Captain George Pollard, Jr., formerly of the *Essex*.

Like many survivors, Pollard was animated by a fierce and desperate compulsion to tell his story: how his ship had been attacked "in a most deliberate manner" by a large sperm whale; how they had headed south in the whaleboats; how his boat had been attacked once again, this time by "an unknown fish"; and how they had found an island where a "few fowl and fish was the only sustenance." He told them that three men still remained on the island. He told of how the rest of them had set out for Easter Island and how Matthew Joy had been the first to die. He told of how Chase's boat had become separated from them in the night and how, in rapid succession, four black men "became food for the remainder." Then he told how, after separating from the second mate's boat, he and his crew "were reduced to the deplorable necessity of casting lots." He told of how the lot fell to Owen Coffin, "who with composure and resignation submitted to his fate." Lastly he told of the death of Barzillai Ray, and how Ray's corpse had kept both him and Ramsdell alive.

Later that night, once he had returned to the *Diana*, Captain Paddack wrote it all down, calling Pollard's account "the most distressing narrative that ever came to my knowledge." The question now became one of how the survivors would fare in the dark shadow of their story.

13

HOMECOMING

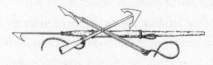

On February 25, 1821, Chase, Lawrence, and Nickerson arrived in Valparaiso, Chile's largest port, set on a steep hill facing north across a wide bay. At any other time the story of the *Essex* would have captivated the city. But in February and March of that year, the citizens of Valparaiso were tensely awaiting news from the north. Revolutionary forces, having already secured Chile's independence from Spain, were bearing down on Royalists in Lima. It was Peru, not a few American castaways, that demanded Valparaiso's attention, allowing the *Essex* survivors to recuperate in relative privacy.

From the beginning Chase and his men spoke openly about having resorted to cannibalism. On the day of the Nantucketers' arrival, the keeper of the port's official log of incoming and outgoing vessels matter-of-factly reported that the captain of the *Indian* had picked up three men who "survived with a little water and crackers . . . and with a shipmate that died and that they ate in the term of eight days."

The U.S. frigate *Constellation* was anchored at Valparaiso, and the acting American consul, Henry Hill, arranged to have Chase, Lawrence, and Nickerson taken to it. Even though it had been a week since their rescue, the survivors still presented an affecting sight. "[T]heir appearance . . . was truly distressing," wrote Commodore Charles Goodwin Ridgely, commander of the *Constellation*, "bones working through their skins, their legs and feet much smaller and the whole surface of their bodies one entire ulcer." Ridgely placed the three men under the care of his surgeon, Dr. Leonard Osborn, who supervised their recovery in the frigate's sick bay deep in the forward part of the third deck. It may have been hot and airless, but for three men who had spent eighty-nine consecutive days beneath the open sky, it was a wonderful comfort.

The crew of the *Constellation* was so profoundly moved by the sufferings of Chase and his men that each sailor donated a dollar toward their assistance. When this was combined with money collected from the American and British residents of Valparaiso, the *Essex* survivors had more than $500.

The day after their arrival in Valparaiso, Chase and his men received a visit from the governor, who had heard rumors that, instead of being the survivors of a wreck, the first mate and his men had killed the *Essex*'s captain in a bloody mutiny. "For there was a whispering abroad," Nickerson wrote, "that foul play had been used by us." The governor was reassured enough by Chase's story that he allowed the Nantucketers to go freely about the city as soon as they were able.

A week and a half later, on March 9, the Nantucket whaleship *Hero* arrived in Valparaiso. While cutting in a whale off St. Mary's Island, she'd been attacked by Spanish pirates. The Spaniards imprisoned the captain and the cabin boy onshore, then locked the rest of the crew belowdecks and began to ransack the ship. When an unknown vessel appeared in the harbor, the pirates returned briefly to shore, allowing first mate Obed Starbuck to burst open the cabin door and retake the ship. Starbuck ordered his men to set sail, and although the pirates came to within yards of catching up to the fleeing whaleship, the Nantucketers were able to reach safety.

As dramatic as that report was, the *Hero* bore even more sensational news. With mate Starbuck acting as skipper, the *Hero* had encountered three whaleships sailing together as an informal group—the *Dauphin*, the *Diana*, and the *Two Brothers*. Captain Zimri Coffin of the *Dauphin* told Starbuck that he had the captain of the *Essex* and another crew member aboard. Shortly afterward, Pollard and Ramsdell were transferred to the *Two Brothers*, which was headed for Valparaiso.

It arrived on March 17. The five survivors had last seen one another on the night of January 12, when their boats had become separated in a howling gale more than two thousand miles out to sea. Since then, two of Chase's crew had died, three of Pollard's, and three of Joy's (then under Hendricks's leadership) before the second mate's boat containing Obed Hendricks, William Bond, and Joseph West disappeared. Only Nantucketers had emerged from Pollard's and Chase's whaleboats alive.

They had all suffered terribly, but it was Pollard and Ramsdell—found clutching the bones of their dead companions—who had come the closest to complete psychic disintegration. Of the anguish each of these two experienced, Pollard's was perhaps the greater. A year and a half earlier, his aunt had entrusted him with the care and protection of her oldest son, Owen. Pollard had not only presided over his cousin's execution but had eaten his flesh, thus participating in what one historian of cannibalism at sea has called the taboo of "gastronomic incest."

Pollard had demonstrated remarkable stamina immediately after his rescue, but his urgent need to tell his tale had almost killed him. Soon after that first night, he suffered a relapse. When Captain William Coffin of the Nantucket whaleship *Eagle* offered the *Essex* survivors passage home, Pollard was judged to be too weak for a voyage around Cape Horn. On March 23, Chase, Lawrence, Nickerson, and Ramsdell bid farewell to their captain and left for Nantucket. In May, after two months of recuperation and solitary reflection, Pollard followed them in the whaleship *Two Brothers*.

➤   ➤   ➤

In the meantime, Commodore Ridgely, commander of the *Constellation*, had made arrangements for the rescue of Chappel, Weeks, and

Wright from (as he was told) Ducie Island. Recently arrived in
Valparaiso was the *Surry*, a trading vessel from Australia being loaded
with 1,500 bushels of wheat. Her captain, Thomas Raine, agreed to stop
at Ducie on his way back to Sydney and pick up the three *Essex* crew
members, assuming they were still alive.

The *Surry* left South America on March 10. Captain Raine and his
crew arrived at Ducie Island less than a month later, only to find the
tiny coral island uninhabited. The shore was so thick with nesting birds
it was impossible to walk without stepping on eggs. Raine decided that
no one had visited this necklace of coral in a very long time.

He studied his navigational guide and wondered if the *Essex* officers might have mistaken an island seventy miles to the west for Ducie.
A few days later, on April 9, Henderson Island came within view.
They approached it from the east, then began to follow the coastline
to the north. Upon rounding a rocky headland they found a "spacious
bay" to the west. Raine ordered one of his men to fire a gun.

➤   ➤   ➤

At that moment, Chappel, Weeks, and Wright had just sat down to eat
a tropic bird. Except for some berries and shellfish, birds and eggs were
the only food left on Henderson. The landcrabs had disappeared. A
few months before, the men had succeeded in catching five green turtles, but by the time they had eaten just one of the turtles, the meat on
the other four had spoiled. Over the last four months, the tropic birds
had proved exceptionally difficult to find, so the bird they had now
was, for them, a bountiful feast. But food was not their gravest concern. What they still needed most was water.

From the day after their seventeen shipmates left for Easter Island,
the spring of freshwater never again emerged above the tide line. At
low tide they could see freshwater bubbling up to the ocean's surface
from the rock, but for the rest of their time on Henderson the spring
always remained covered by saltwater.

In desperation, Chappel, Weeks, and Wright dug a series of wells but were unable to reach groundwater. When it rained, they would greedily collect the water that accumulated in the hollows of nearby rocks. Dehydration caused their tongues to swell and their lips to crack. After a five-day stretch without water, they reluctantly sucked the blood of a tropic bird but found themselves "much disordered" by it. While searching the crevices and caves for water, they discovered the remains of the eight unidentified castaways, whose fate they feared would soon be their own. The skeletons lay side by side as if the people had decided to lie down and quietly die together. For Chappel, who had once been the wildest and least responsible of the Essex's crew, it was a sight that helped change his life. From that day forward, he would look to God. "I found religion not only useful," he later wrote, "but absolutely necessary to enable me to bear up under these severe trials."

When Chappel, Weeks, and Wright, crouched around their tropic-bird feast, heard a distant booming, they assumed it was thunder, but one of the men decided to walk down to the beach and have a look. Later he would tell what had happened as soon as he saw the ship: "The poor fellow," one of the Surry's crew members reported, "was so overpowered with the emotions such a sight excited in his breast, he could not go to tell his companions the joyful news." Finally, however, they, too, grew curious and joined him at the beach.

A high surf was breaking on the ledge of coral surrounding the island. Several times the crew of the Surry attempted to land a boat, but the conditions proved too dangerous. The three desperate men stood on the beach, increasingly fearful that their rescuers would decide to abandon them. Finally Chappel, the strongest of the three and the only one who knew how to swim, dove into the sea. His arms were skin and bone but with the adrenaline coursing through him, he reached the launch and was pulled aboard.

The rescue from Henderson Island, from *An Account of the Loss of the* Essex by Thomas Chappel.

The *Surry*'s crew discussed what to do next. They might have to return the following day for the other two men. But Chappel refused to abandon his two shipmates even temporarily. With a rope tied around his waist, he dove into the water and swam back over the coral to the beach. One at a time, the three of them were pulled out to the boat. They suffered many cuts and bruises from the reef, but all made it to the *Surry* alive.

Captain Raine judged that the three of them would have been dead after another month on the island. Their clothes were mere rags; between them they had only a single pair of pants. Somehow one of them had been able to save his seaman's certificate, on which he had kept a record of their days spent on Henderson. They told Raine that Captain Pollard had left several letters in a box nailed to a tree, and the next day Raine was able to land on the island and retrieve the letters.

They are all safe

➤   ➤   ➤

The only *Essex* crew members not accounted for were the three men—Obed Hendricks, Joseph West, and William Bond—in the second mate's boat, which separated from Pollard's on the night of January 29. Months later, long after Captain Raine had searched Ducie Island, the atoll to the east of Henderson, another ship touched down there. The crew discovered a whaleboat washed up on the brittle shore, with four skeletons inside. In 1825 the British navy captain Frederick William Beechey, who visited both Ducie and Henderson islands, made the connection between this ghostly vessel of bones and the lost *Essex* boat. If this was indeed the second mate's whaleboat and the skeletons belonged to Hendricks, West, Bond, and perhaps Isaiah Sheppard, the last of the crew to die before the separation from Pollard, then it had drifted for more than a thousand miles, finally coming to rest within a day's sail of where it had started on December 27, 1820.

➤   ➤   ➤

The families of the *Essex* crew members had no reason for concern throughout the winter and spring. Letters mailed from South America in late October would not have reached Nantucket until February or March at the earliest. They would have told of a typical whaling voyage reaching its midpoint, with hopes high that a productive season in the Offshore Ground would allow them to return home in the summer of 1822.

What the people of Nantucket did not know was that since late February, a kind of tidal wave of horror had been building in the whale fishery as the story of the *Essex* was passed from ship to ship, gradually making its way around the Horn and up the Atlantic toward Nantucket. Riding the crest of this wave was the *Eagle*, with Chase, Lawrence, Nickerson, and Ramsdell aboard. Before the *Eagle*'s arrival, however, a letter reached Nantucket that told of the disaster.

The town's post office was on Main Street, and as soon as the letter arrived, it was read there before an overflowing crowd. The islander Frederick Sanford was a contemporary of the Nantucket teenagers aboard the *Essex*, and he would never forget what he saw and heard that day. The letter, Sanford recalled, told of "their sufferings in the boats, eating each other, and some of them my old playmates at school!" Despite Nantucket's reputation for Quaker stoicism, the people assembled outside the post office could not conceal their emotions. "[E]veryone was overcome by [the letter's] recital," Sanford wrote, "and [wept] in the streets."

As it turned out, the letter contained an incomplete account of the disaster. Pollard and Ramsdell had been rescued almost a week after Chase's boat-crew, but their account—passed from whaleship to whaleship—was the first to make it home. The letter mentioned the three men left on the island but gave little hope for any other survivors. Pollard and Ramsdell were assumed to be the only Nantucketers left alive.

On June 11, the *Eagle* arrived at the Nantucket Bar. "My family had received the most distressing account of our shipwreck," Chase wrote, "and had given me up for lost." But standing alongside Ramsdell was not George Pollard; instead, there were three ghosts—Owen Chase, Benjamin Lawrence, and Thomas Nickerson. Tears of sorrow were soon succeeded by amazement and then tears of joy. "My unexpected appearance," Chase remembered, "was welcomed with the most grateful obligations and acknowledgments to a beneficent Creator, who had guided me through darkness, trouble, and death, once more to the bosom of my country and friends."

Chase discovered that he was the father of a fourteen-month-old daughter, Phebe Ann. For Chase's wife, Peggy, it was an overwhelming sight: the husband whom she had once thought dead holding their chubby-cheeked daughter in his still bony, scab-covered arms.

The community of Nantucket was overwhelmed as well. Obed

Macy, the meticulous keeper of Nantucket's historical record, chose not to mention the disaster in his journal. Although articles quickly appeared about the *Essex* in the *New Bedford Mercury*, Nantucket's own fledgling newspaper, the *Inquirer,* did not write about the disaster that summer. It was as if Nantucketers were refusing to commit to an opinion about the matter until they had first had a chance to hear from the *Essex*'s captain, George Pollard, Jr.

➤ ➤ ➤

They would have to wait almost two months, until August 5, when Pollard returned to the island aboard the *Two Brothers*. The whaleship was first sighted by the lookout posted at the tower of the Congregational church. As word spread down the lanes and into the shops and warehouses and out into the wharves, a crowd formed and began to make its way to the cliff along the north shore. From there they could see the black, sea-worn ship, heavy with oil, her sails furled, anchored at the Nantucket Bar. At 222 tons, the *Two Brothers* was even smaller than the *Essex* had been, and once she'd been relieved of some of her oil, she crossed the Bar at high tide and made her way toward the harbor entrance. The crowd surged back to the waterfront. Soon more than 1,500 people were waiting expectantly at the wharves.

The arrival of a whaleship—any whaleship—was what one Nantucketer called "an era in most of our lives." It was the way people learned about the ones they loved—the sons, husbands, fathers, uncles, and friends whose workplace was on the other side of the world. Since no one knew what news the whaleship might bring, islanders greeting a ship tended to hide their eagerness and anxiety behind a veneer of solemnity. "We feel a singular blending of joy and grief on such occasions," this same Nantucketer confessed. "We know not whether to smile or weep. Our emotion at all events is much subdued. We dare not express it *aloud* lest it grate upon the ear of some to whom this ship has been a harbinger of evil. We are disposed to be quiet. And yet at this time we have an irresistible impulse to *utter* our feelings."

And so, when Pollard first stepped upon the wharf, surrounded by more than a thousand familiar faces, there was an absolute, nerve-shattering quiet. Frederick Sanford, Nickerson's and Ramsdell's old school chum, would later describe the assembly as "an awe-struck, silent crowd." As Pollard began to make his way toward home, people moved aside to let him pass. No one said a word.

As a mate aboard the *Essex*, George Pollard had known only success; as captain, he had known only disaster. Since a whaleman was paid a portion of the proceeds at the end of the voyage, Pollard, like all the other survivors, had nothing to show for two years of misery and hardship except for the relief money raised in Valparaiso.

Pollard was inevitably subjected to a lengthy interview by the *Essex*'s owners, Gideon Folger and Paul Macy, a harrowing process during which it would have been difficult for a first-time captain not to sound defensive. But it wasn't just the *Essex*'s owners to whom Pollard had to answer. There was a member of his own family—Owen Coffin's mother.

➤   ➤   ➤

Nancy Bunker Coffin, forty-three, was Pollard's aunt, the sister of his mother, Tamar, fifty-seven. Pollard's emotions can only be guessed when he arrived on her doorstep. "He bore the awful message to the mother as her son desired," Nickerson wrote. Nancy Coffin did not take it well. The idea that the man to whom she had entrusted the care of her seventeen-year-old son was living as a consequence of her boy's death was too much for her to bear. "[S]he became almost frantic with the thought," Nickerson wrote, "and I have heard that she never could become reconciled to the captain's presence."

The verdict of the community was less harsh. The drawing of lots was accepted by the unwritten law of the sea as permissible in a survival situation. "Captain Pollard was not thought to have dealt unfairly with this trying matter," Nickerson wrote.

For his own part, Pollard did not allow the horror he had experienced in the whaleboat to defeat him, displaying an honesty and directness concerning the disaster that would sustain him all his life. Captain George Worth of the *Two Brothers* was so impressed with the integrity of the former captain of the *Essex* during the two-and-a-half-month voyage back from Valparaiso that he recommended Pollard as his replacement. Soon after his return, Pollard was formally offered command of the *Two Brothers*.

By the time Pollard returned to Nantucket, Owen Chase had begun working on a book about the disaster. Chase had grown up with a boy who, instead of shipping out for the Pacific, had attended Harvard College. William Coffin, Jr., was the twenty-three-year-old son of a successful whale-oil merchant who had also served as Nantucket's first postmaster.

Coffin was the ideal person to work with Chase. Well educated and an accomplished writer, Coffin also had a thorough knowledge of both Nantucket and whaling. Being Chase's own age, he could empathize with the young first mate in a way that makes the narrative read, Melville noted, "as tho' Owen wrote it himself." The two men worked quickly and well together. By early fall the manuscript was finished. By November 22, almost precisely a year after the sinking, the published book had reached shops on Nantucket.

Chase's fellow Nantucket survivors, particularly Captain Pollard, undoubtedly felt that their side of the story had not been adequately told in the first mate's account of the disaster. But it wasn't just Chase's fellow crew members who felt slighted by the publication of the *Essex* narrative. As Ralph Waldo Emerson would observe during a visit to the island in 1847, Nantucketers are "[v]ery sensitive to everything that dishonors the island because it hurts the value of stock till the company are poorer." The last thing they wanted placed before the nation and the world was a detailed account of how some of their own men and boys had been reduced to cannibalism. Chase's account pulled no punches on this issue, employing two exclamation marks when it came to the initial proposal to eat Isaac Cole. No matter how bad a man's circumstances, many believed, he should not attempt to enrich himself by sensationalizing the sufferings of his own people. Significantly, Chase's next voyage would not be on a Nantucket whaleship. That December he traveled to New Bedford, where he sailed as first mate on the *Florida*, a whaleship without a single Nantucketer in the crew. Even though his family remained on the island, Chase would not sail on a ship from his home port for another eleven years.

George Pollard, however, was given the ultimate vote of confidence. On November 26, 1821, a little more than three months after returning to Nantucket and just a few days after the appearance of Chase's narrative, he set sail for the Pacific as captain of the *Two Brothers*. But perhaps the most extraordinary endorsement Pollard received came from two of his crew members. For Pollard wasn't the only *Essex* man aboard the *Two Brothers;* two others had chosen to serve under him again. One was Thomas Nickerson. The other was Charles Ramsdell, the boy who had spent ninety-four days in a whaleboat with him. If there was someone who had come to know Captain Pollard, it was Charles Ramsdell.

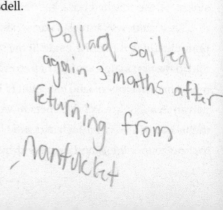

Pollard sailed again 3 months after returning from Nantucket

14

CONSEQUENCES

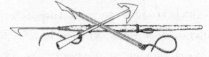

George Pollard took to his second command with optimism that was remarkable, considering what had happened to his first. In the winter of 1822 he successfully brought the *Two Brothers* around Cape Horn, headed her up the west coast of South America, and provisioned her at the Peruvian port of Payta. In mid-August the *Two Brothers* spoke the U.S. Navy schooner *Waterwitch*. Aboard the *Waterwitch* was a twenty-four-year-old midshipman named Charles Wilkes. As it so happened, Wilkes had read a newspaper account of the *Essex* disaster. Wilkes asked Pollard how, after all that he had suffered, he could dare go to sea again. "He simply remarked," Wilkes wrote, "that it was an old adage that the lightning never struck in the same place twice." But in the case of Captain Pollard, it did.

In February of 1823 the *Two Brothers* and another Nantucket whaleship, the *Martha*, were sailing west together toward a new whaling ground. In the few years since the start of Pollard's previous voyage, much had changed in the Pacific whale fishery. Soon after the opening up of the Offshore Ground in 1819, Nantucket whaleships had stopped at the Hawaiian island of Oahu for the first time. That same year, Frederick Coffin, captain of the *Syren*, laid claim to discovering the rich Japan Ground. All of the Pacific, not just its eastern and western edges, had become the domain of the Nantucket whalemen.

The *Two Brothers* and the *Martha* were several hundred miles west of the Hawaiian Islands, headed toward the Japan Ground, when it began to blow. Pollard ordered his men to shorten sail. It was raining hard, and in the high seas, the *Two Brothers* was proving difficult to steer. The *Martha* was the faster of the two whaleships, and as night came on, the lookout of the *Two Brothers* could barely see her from the masthead.

They were sailing at about the same latitude as French Frigate Shoals—a deadly maze of rocks and coral reefs to the northwest of the Hawaiian Islands—but both Pollard and Captain John Pease of the *Martha* judged themselves to be well to the west of danger. Since his previous voyage, Pollard had learned how to determine his ship's longitude by lunar observation. However, owing to overcast skies, it had been more than ten days since he had been able to take a lunar, so he had to rely on dead reckoning to determine his ship's position.

It was blowing so hard that the whaleboats had been taken off the davits and lashed to the deck. That night one of the officers remarked that "the water alongside looked whiter than usual." Thomas Nickerson was about to retrieve a jacket from down below when he noticed Pollard standing on the ship's railing, staring down worriedly into the sea.

While Nickerson was belowdecks, the ship struck something "with a fearful crash," and he was thrown to the floor. Nickerson assumed they had collided with another ship. "Judge of my astonishment," he wrote, "to find ourselves surrounded with breakers apparently mountains high, and our ship careening over upon her broadside and thumping so heavily that one could scarcely stand upon his feet." The ship was being pounded to pieces on a coral reef. "Captain Pollard seemed to stand amazed at the scene before him," Nickerson remembered.

First mate Eben Gardner took charge. He ordered the men to begin cutting down the masts in hopes of saving the ship. Realizing that the spars would likely fall across and crush the whaleboats tied to the deck, Pollard finally came to life. He commanded the crew to put away their axes and begin readying the boats. "Had the masts of the ship been cut away at that time," Nickerson wrote, "[I] would probably have adorned this tale instead of [told] it."

But by the time the men begun crowding into the two boats, Pollard had lapsed into his former state of mesmerized despair. "[H]is reasoning powers had flown," Nickerson remembered, and the captain appeared unwilling to leave the ship. The waves threatened to bash the boats against the hull as the men pleaded with their commander to save himself. "Captain Pollard reluctantly got into the boat," Nickerson wrote, "just as they were about to shove off from the ship."

Nickerson, who at seventeen years old had been promoted to boat-steerer, was standing at the steering oar when a huge wave slammed into the boat and threw him into the sea. One of the mates reached out to him with the blade of the after oar. Nickerson grabbed it and was pulled back into the boat.

The two whaleboats were quickly separated in the darkness. "Our boat seemed to be surrounded with breakers," Nickerson remembered, "and we were compelled to row between them all night for we could see no outlet." The next morning they saw a ship anchored in the lee of a fifty-foot-high rock. It proved to be the *Martha*, which had narrowly escaped crashing into the rock the night before. Soon all of the *Two Brothers'* crew had been rescued, and the *Martha* was on her way to Oahu.

➤   ➤   ➤

Two months later, in the harbor of Raiatea, one of the Society Islands, a missionary named George Bennet boarded the U.S. brig *Pearl* bound for Boston. Among the passengers was George Pollard. The thirty-one-year-old captain had greatly changed since he'd talked to Charles Wilkes less than a year before. His former cheerfulness had disappeared. Yet, anchored in the harbor of an island that he and his men had once spurned in the mistaken fear of cannibals, he insisted on telling Bennet the story of the *Essex* in painful detail. This time, when it came to describing the execution of Owen Coffin, he broke off. "But I can tell you no more," he cried out to Bennet, "my head is on fire at the recollection; I hardly know what I say."

Pollard finished the conversation by relating how he had recently lost his second whaleship on a shoal off the Hawaiian Islands. Then, in what Bennet called "a tone of despondency never to be forgotten by him who heard it," Pollard confessed, "[N]ow I am utterly ruined. No owner will ever trust me with a whaler again, for all will say I am an *unlucky* man."

As Pollard predicted, his whaling career was over. The island that had rallied so quickly behind him after the sinking of the *Essex* now turned its back. He had become a Jonah—a twice-doomed captain whom no one dared give a third chance. After returning to his wife, Mary, Pollard made a single voyage in a merchant vessel out of New York. "[B]ut not liking that business," Nickerson wrote, "he returned to his home on Nantucket." He became a night watchman—a position on the lowest rung of the island's social ladder.

> > >

As a whaleman, Owen Chase would enjoy the success that had eluded George Pollard. His personal life, however, proved less fortunate.

Chase's first voyage after the sinking of the *Essex*, as first mate aboard the New Bedford whaleship *Florida*, lasted less than two years and reaped two thousand barrels of oil. When he returned to Nantucket in 1823, he found a second child, Lydia, toddling after her older sister, Phebe Ann, now approaching four. Chase chose to remain on-island for the birth of his next child, a son, who was named William Henry. Owen's wife, Peggy, did not recover from the delivery. She died less than two weeks later. Owen was now a twenty-seven-year-old widower with three children to care for.

In the fall and winter of 1824–25 he came to know a woman with whom he already shared a special bond. Nancy Slade Joy was the widow of Matthew Joy, second mate of the *Essex*. In June of 1825, nine months after the death of Peggy Chase, the widow and widower were married, and Nancy became the stepmother of Owen's three children. In early August, Chase sailed for New Bedford, where he took command of his first vessel, the *Winslow*.

The *Winslow* was a small whaleship and carried only fifteen men. On July 20, 1827, after a voyage of almost two years, she returned to New Bedford with 1,440 barrels of oil. After a brief reunion with his family on Nantucket, Chase was back in New Bedford by the second week in August, preparing for another voyage.

Chase's almost decade-long professional banishment from Nantucket ended in 1830 soon after his return from his second full voyage as captain of the *Winslow*. At the age of thirty-three he was offered command of what was to be one of the largest ships in the Nantucket whale fishery. Until then, almost all the island's ships were built on the mainland in places such as Rochester and Hanover, Massachusetts. But whaling had brought a tremendous surge of wealth to the island. The profit margins were now high enough that it was deemed economically feasible to build a whaleship at the island's Brant Point Shipyard, even though all the materials had to be transported across Nantucket Sound. Over the next two years, the 376-ton, copper-fastened whaleship *Charles Carroll* took shape under Chase's experienced eye, and with an investment of $625 he was given a 1/32 owners' share in the vessel.

Chase's first voyage as captain of the *Charles Carroll* was a financial success. After three and a half years, he returned in March 1836 with 2,610 barrels of oil, almost twice the return of his first voyage as captain aboard the *Winslow*. But the voyage came at a great personal cost. Nine months after her husband left the island, Nancy Chase gave birth to a daughter, Adeline. A few weeks later, Nancy was dead.

Greeting their father at the wharf in the spring of 1836 were Phebe Ann, almost sixteen; Lydia, thirteen; William Henry, eleven; and Adeline, two and a half—a girl who had no memory of her mother and had never known her father.

Chase wasn't home a month before he had remarried. Eunice Chadwick was just twenty-seven years old, and she now had four stepchildren to care for. By the end of August, after less than five months of marriage, she was waving good-bye to her new husband. This was to be Chase's last voyage as a whaling captain. He was forty years old and, if all went well, would be able to retire to his house on Orange Street.

> > >

Also in the Pacific during this period was a young man whose whaling career was just beginning. Herman Melville first signed on in 1840 as a hand aboard the New Bedford whaleship *Acushnet*. During a gam in the Pacific, he met a Nantucketer by the name of William Henry Chase—Owen Chase's teenage son. Melville had already heard stories about the *Essex* from the sailors aboard the *Acushnet* and closely questioned the boy about his father's experiences. The next morning William pulled out a copy of Owen's *Essex* narrative from his sea chest and loaned it to Melville. "The reading of this wondrous story upon the landless sea," Melville remembered, "and so close to the very latitude of the shipwreck had a surprising effect upon me."

Later in the voyage, during a gam with another whaleship, Melville caught a glimpse of a Nantucket whaling captain who he was told was none other than Owen Chase. "He was a large, powerful well-made man," Melville would later write in the back pages of his own copy of Chase's narrative, "rather tall; to all appearances something past forty-five or so; with a handsome face for a Yankee, and expressive of great uprightness and calm unostentatious courage. His whole appearance impressed me pleasantly. He was the most prepossessing-looking whalehunter I think I ever saw." Although Melville appears to have mistaken another whaling captain for Chase, his description is remarkably similar to a surviving portrait of Owen Chase. It depicts a confident, almost arrogant face—a man completely at ease with the responsibility of command. But Chase's professional assurance would not prepare him for the news he heard midway through his final voyage.

➤   ➤   ➤

Sixteen months after her husband sailed aboard the *Charles Carroll*, Eunice Chase, Owen Chase's third wife, gave birth to a son, Charles Frederick. Herman Melville would be told of how Chase received the news, and inevitably the future author of *Moby-Dick* would compare the plight of the former first mate of the *Essex* to that of George Pollard. "The miserable pertinaciousness of misfortune which pursued Pollard the captain, in his second disastrous and entire shipwreck did likewise hunt poor Owen," Melville wrote, "tho' somewhat more dilatory in overtaking him the second time." Melville was told that Chase had received letters "informing him of the certain infidelity of his wife. . . . We also heard that his receipt of this news had told most heavily upon Chase, and that he was a prey to the deepest gloom."

A matter of days after his return to Nantucket in the winter of 1840, Chase filed for divorce. On July 7, the divorce was granted, with Chase taking over legal guardianship of Charles Frederick. Two months later, Chase was married for the fourth time, to Susan Coffin Gwinn. In the previous twenty-one years, he had spent only five at home. He would now remain on Nantucket for the rest of his life.

➤   ➤   ➤

The other *Essex* survivors also returned to the sea. Once they'd been delivered to Oahu after the wreck of the *Two Brothers*, Thomas Nickerson and Charles Ramsdell soon found berths on other whaleships. In the 1840s Ramsdell served as captain of the *General Jackson* out of

Bristol, Rhode Island; he would marry twice and have a total of six children. Nickerson eventually tired of the whaling life and became a captain in the merchant service, relocating to Brooklyn, New York, where he and his wife, Margaret, lived for a number of years. They had no children.

Benjamin Lawrence served as captain of the whaleships *Dromo* and *Huron,* the latter out of Hudson, New York, home of the *Essex*'s second mate, Matthew Joy. Lawrence had seven children, one of whom would die at sea. In the early 1840s, Lawrence, like Chase, retired from the whaling business and purchased a small farm at Siasconset, on the east end of the island of Nantucket.

Less is known about the three off-islanders rescued from Henderson Island. The two Cape Codders, Seth Weeks and William Wright, continued as crew members on the *Surry,* voyaging throughout the Pacific until they made their way to England and back to the United States. Wright was lost at sea in a hurricane off the West Indies. Weeks eventually retired to Cape Cod, where he would outlive all the other *Essex* survivors.

The Englishman Thomas Chappel returned to London in June 1823. There he contributed to a religious tract that wrung every possible spiritual lesson from the story of the *Essex* disaster. Nickerson later heard of the Englishman's death on the fever-plagued island of Timor.

➤   ➤   ➤

Although townspeople continued to whisper about the *Essex* well into the twentieth century, it was not a topic a Nantucketer openly discussed. When the daughter of Benjamin Lawrence was asked about the disaster, she replied, "We do not mention this in Nantucket."

By 1835, when Obed Macy published, with the assistance of William Coffin, Jr., his *History of Nantucket,* New Bedford had eclipsed the island as America's leading whaling port. The Nantucket Bar—a mere nuisance in the early days of the Pacific whale fishery—

had developed into a major obstacle to prosperity. The whaleships had become so large that they could no longer cross the Bar without being almost completely unloaded by smaller vessels known as lighters—a time-consuming and expensive process. In 1842, Peter Folger Ewer designed and built two 135-foot "camels"—giant wooden water wings that formed a floating dry dock capable of carrying a fully loaded whaleship across the Bar. The fact remained, however, that New Bedford's deep-water harbor gave the port a distinct advantage, as did its nearness to the newly emerging railroad system, on which increasing numbers of merchants shipped their oil to market.

But Nantucketers also had themselves to blame for the dramatic downturn the whaling business would take on the island in the 1840s. As whalemen from New Bedford, New London, and Sag Harbor opened up new whaling grounds in the North Pacific, Nantucketers stuck stubbornly to the long-since depleted grounds that had served them so well in past decades.

Long before Edwin Drake struck oil in Titusville, Pennsylvania, in 1859, Nantucket's economic fate had been determined. Over the next twenty years, the island's population would shrink from 10,000 to 3,000. "Nantucket now has a 'body-o'-death' appearance such as few New England towns possess," one visitor wrote. "The houses stand around in faded gentility style—the inhabitants have a dreamy look, as though they live in the memories of the past." Even though whaling would continue out of New Bedford into the 1920s, Nantucket, the island whose name had once been synonymous with the fishery, had ceased to be an active whaling port only forty years after the departure of the *Essex*. On November 16, 1869, Nantucket's last whaling vessel, the *Oak*, left the harbor, never to return.

➤   ➤   ➤

Nantucket, once the whaling capital of the world, was all but a ghost town by the time the last survivors of the *Essex* disaster began to pass away. Charles Ramsdell was the first of the Nantucketers to die, in 1866. Throughout his life he was known for his reticence concerning the *Essex*, in part, one islander thought, because of his role as Owen Coffin's executioner.

Old age was not kind to Owen Chase. His memory of his sufferings in an open boat never left him, and late in life he began hiding food in the attic of his house on Orange Street. By 1868 Chase was judged "insane." The headaches that had plagued him ever since the ordeal had become unbearable. Clutching an attendant's hand, he would sob, "Oh my head, my head." Death brought an end to Chase's suffering in 1869.

George Pollard followed his former first mate the next year. The obituary was careful to note that Pollard had been known on the island as something more than the captain of the *Essex*: "For more than forty years he has resided permanently among us; and leaves a record of a good and worthy man as his legacy."

In the 1870s, Thomas Nickerson returned to Nantucket and moved into a house on North Water Street, not far from where his parents were buried in the Old North Burial Ground. Instead of whales, Nantucketers were now after summer visitors, and Nickerson developed a reputation as one of the island's foremost boardinghouse keepers. One of his guests was the writer Leon Lewis, who, after hearing Nickerson tell about the *Essex*, proposed that they collaborate on a book about the disaster.

Nickerson had talked with Charles Ramsdell about his experiences in the whaleboat with Pollard; he had also spoken with Seth Weeks on Cape Cod about his time on Henderson Island. As a consequence, Nickerson's narrative provides information that was unavailable to Chase. He also includes important details about the voyage prior to the whale attack. But Nickerson, like Chase before him, was not above adjusting his account to suit his own purposes. Not wanting to be remembered as a cannibal, he claims that the men in Chase's boat did not eat the body of Isaac Cole. Instead, he insists, it was the extra bread made available to them by the deaths of Cole and Peterson that "enabled us to exist until relieved." He also chose not to recount how, toward the end of the ordeal, he suddenly decided it was his turn to die.

In April 1879, Nickerson's last surviving crew member in the first mate's boat, Benjamin Lawrence, died. All his life, Lawrence had kept the piece of twine he'd made while in the whaleboat. At some point it was passed on to Alexander Starbuck, the Nantucketer who had taken over Obed Macy's role as the island's historian. In 1914, Starbuck would donate the piece of twine, wound four times into a tiny coil and mounted in a frame, to the Nantucket Historical Association. Written within the circle of twine was the inscription "They were in the Boat 93 Days."

Eighteen years earlier, in 1896, the Nantucket Historical Association had received another donation associated with the *Essex*. Sometime after the ship sank in November 1820, a small chest, ten by twenty inches, was found floating in the vicinity of the wreck. Leather-bound and studded with brass nails, it may have been used by Captain Pollard to store the ship's papers. It was picked up by the crew of a passing ship and sold to John Taber, a whaleman then on his way home to Providence, Rhode Island. In 1896, Taber's daughter, who had since moved to Garrettsville, Ohio, decided that the chest rightfully belonged on Nantucket and donated the artifact to the historical association.

It was all that remained of the whaleship *Essex*—a battered box and a ragged piece of string.

EPILOGUE

Nantucket has changed greatly in recent decades. What was a generation or so ago a decrepit fishing village with a famous past and a few tourists in July and August has become a thriving summer resort. After a century of neglect, downtown Nantucket has been restored. Instead of sail lofts, grocers, and barbershops, however, the buildings now house art galleries, designer clothing boutiques, and T-shirt shops, all of which would have appalled the good gray Quakers of the whaling era. Spurning the cobblestoned elegance of Main Street, Nantucket's latest crop of millionaires build their "trophy houses" by the beach. People still gaze from the tower of the Congregational church, but instead of scanning the horizon for oil-laden whaleships, the tourists—who have paid two dollars to sweat their way up the ninety-four steps to the belfry—watch high-speed ferries bringing cargoes of day-trippers from Cape Cod.

At the height of its influence more than 150 years ago, Nantucket had led the new nation toward its destiny as a world power. "Let America add Mexico to Texas, and pile Cuba upon Canada," Melville wrote in *Moby-Dick*, "let the English overswarm all India, and lay out their blazing banner from the sun; two thirds of this terraqueous globe are the Nantucketer's." But if the island's inhabitants once ventured to the far corners of the world, today it seems as if the world has made its way to Nantucket. It is not whaling, of course, that brings the tourists to the island, but the romantic glorification of whaling—the same kind of myths that historically important places all across America have learned to shine and polish to their economic advantage. Yet, despite the circus (some have called it a theme park) that is modern Nantucket, the story of the *Essex* is too troubling, too complex to fit comfortably into a chamber of commerce brochure.

Unlike, say, Sir Ernest Shackleton and his men, who by journeying to Antarctica put themselves in harm's way and then had the luck to live out a fantasy of male camaraderie and heroism, Captain Pollard and his crew were simply attempting to make a living when disaster struck in the form of an eighty-five-foot whale. After that, they did the best they could. Mistakes were inevitably made. While Captain Pollard's instincts were sound, he did not have the strength of character to impose his will on his two younger officers. Instead of sailing to Tahiti and safety, they set out on an impossible voyage, wandering the watery desert of the Pacific until most of them were dead. Like the Donner party, the men of the *Essex* could have avoided disaster, but this does not diminish the extent of the men's sufferings, or their bravery and extraordinary discipline.

Some have praised the officers of the *Essex* for their navigational skills, but it was their seamanship, their ability to keep their little boats upright and sailing for three months in the open ocean, that is even more astonishing. Captain Bligh and his men sailed almost as far, but they had the coast of Australia and a string of islands to follow, along with favorable winds. Bligh's voyage lasted forty-eight days; the *Essex* boats were out for almost twice as long.

From the beginning the Nantucketers in the crew took measures to provide one another with the greatest possible support without blatantly compromising the safety of the others. Although rations appear to have been distributed equally, it was almost as if the Nantucketers existed in a protective bubble as off-island crew members, first black then white, fell by the wayside until the Nantucketers had, in the case of Pollard's crew, no choice but to eat their own. The *Essex* disaster is not a tale of adventure. It is a tragedy that happens to be one of the greatest true stories ever told.

FURTHER READING

For more information about the *Essex*, Nantucket, and other related topics, here are some interesting resources:

Ashley, Clifford W. *The Yankee Whaler*. Boston: Houghton Mifflin, 1926. A fun, in-depth account of whaling written by a man who actually did it as a boy.

Ellis, Richard. *Men and Whales*. New York: Knopf, 1991. An excellent guide to whales and whaling.

Heffernan, Thomas. *Stove by a Whale: Owen Chase and the* Essex. Hanover, N.H.: University Press of New England, 1990. An analysis of the *Essex* disaster from the perspective of Owen Chase.

Macy, Obed. *The History of Nantucket*. 1835. Reprint, Ellinwood, Kan.: Macys of Ellinwood, 1985. The first history of the island published in 1835. A surprisingly good read.

Macy, William F. *The Nantucket Scrap-Basket*. 1916. Reprint, Ellinwood, Kan.: Macys of Ellinwood, 1984. A book of anecdotes and sayings from Nantucket—great and informative reading.

Melville, Herman. *Moby-Dick, or The Whale*. 1851. Reprint, New York: Penguin, 2001. The ultimate American novel about whaling. It's long, but it's worth it.

Nickerson, Thomas; Chase, Owen; and Others. *The Loss of the Ship* Essex, *Sunk by a Whale*. New York: Penguin, 2000. This contains most of the primary sources I used in writing *Revenge of the Whale*. It includes all of Nickerson's and Chase's narratives and much more.

Philbrick, Nathaniel. *Away Off Shore: Nantucket Island and Its People, 1602– 1890*. Nantucket, Mass.: Mill Hill Press, 1994. A history of Nantucket with a chapter about the *Essex* disaster.

————. *Abram's Eyes: The Native American Legacy of Nantucket Island*. Nantucket, Mass.: Mill Hill Press, 1998. The Native American history of the island, with an epilogue that compares the story of the *Essex* disaster to the Wampanoag myth of the giant Maushop.

Read, Piers Paul. *Alive!: The Story of the Andes Survivors*. New York: Avon, 1975. The story of an airplane crash and survival ordeal with many grisly parallels to the *Essex*.

Stackpole, Edouard. *The Loss of the* Essex, *Sunk by a Whale in Mid-Ocean*. Falmouth, Mass.: Kendall Printing, 1977. A good, brief account of the *Essex* disaster, written by Nantucket's foremost whaling historian and the man who first discovered Nickerson's journal in 1980.

INDEX

TURN THE PAGE FOR A PREVIEW OF

THE GRIPPING, TRUE STORY OF HOW

OUR NATION WAS FOUNDED.

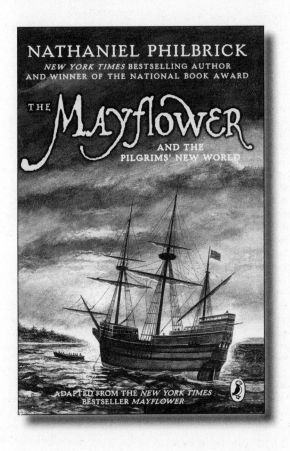

PREFACE
The Story We Need to Know

• • •

WE'VE ALL HEARD at least some version of the story of the *Mayflower*, how in 1620 the Pilgrims sailed to the New World in search of religious freedom; how after drawing up the Mayflower Compact, they landed at Plymouth Rock and befriended the local Wampanoag Indians, who taught them how to plant corn and whose leader, or sachem, Massasoit, helped them celebrate the First Thanksgiving.

But the story of the Pilgrims does not end with the First Thanksgiving. When we look at how the Pilgrims and the Wampanoags maintained more than fifty years of peace and how that peace suddenly erupted into King Philip's War, one of the deadliest wars ever fought on American soil, the real history of Plymouth Colony becomes something altogether new, rich, troubling, and complex. Instead of the story we already know, it becomes the story we *need* to know.

• • • It was King Philip who led me to the Pilgrims. Philip was the son of Massasoit, the Wampanoag leader who formed an alliance with the Pilgrims in 1621. I was researching the history of my adopted home, Nantucket Island, when I encountered a reference to Philip in the town's records. In attempting to answer the question of why Philip—whose headquarters were in modern Bristol, Rhode Island—had traveled more than sixty-five miles across the water to Nantucket, I realized that I had to begin with Philip's father, Massasoit, and the Pilgrims.

My first impression of the period consisted of two conflicting ideas: the time-honored tradition of how the Pilgrims came to symbolize all that is good about America, and the now equally familiar modern tale of how the evil Europeans killed the innocent Native Americans. I soon learned that the real-life Indians and English of the seventeenth century were too smart, too generous, too greedy, too brave—in short, too human—to behave so predictably.

Without Massasoit's help, the Pilgrims would never have survived their first year in America, and they remained supporters of the sachem to the very end. For his part, Massasoit realized almost from the start that his own fortunes were linked to those of the English. In this respect, there is a surprising amount of truth in the traditional story of the First Thanksgiving.

But the Indians and English of Plymouth Colony did not live in perfect harmony. It was fifty-five years of struggle and compromise—a difficult process of give-and-take. As long as both sides recognized that they needed each other, there was peace. The moment any of them gave up on the difficult work of living with their neighbors, they risked losing everything. It was a lesson that the first generation of Plymouth Colony had learned over the course of more than three long decades. That it could be so quickly forgotten by their children remains a lesson for us today.

King Philip's War lasted only fourteen months, but it changed the face of New England. After fifty-five years of peace, the lives of Native and English peoples had become so closely intertwined that when fighting broke out in June 1675, many of the region's Indians found themselves, in the words of a contemporary writer, "in a kind of maze, not knowing what to do."

Some Indians chose to support Philip; others joined the colonial forces; still others attempted to stay out of the conflict altogether. When the English authorities decided that all Indians—no matter whose side they said they were on—were now their enemies, the violence quickly spread. Soon, the entire region was a terrifying war zone. By the end of the fighting, a third of the hundred or so towns in New England had been burned and abandoned.

When violence and fear grip a society, there is an almost overpowering temptation to demonize the enemy, and both Indians and English began to view their former neighbors as subhuman and evil. But even in the midst of one of the deadliest wars in American history, there were Englishmen who believed the Indians were not naturally evil, and there were Indians who believed the same about the English. They remembered to treat each other like human beings and to keep learning from each other, just as their parents had done fifty years before. Unfortunately, this was not enough to prevent war from destroying the promise of the First Thanksgiving.

◆ ◆ ◆ The story of the *Mayflower* ends in tragedy, but it begins with a ship on a wide and blustery sea.